How To Bounce Back From Adversity

Linda G. Hodge

WINNING IN LIFE: BOUNCING BACK FROM ADVERSITY
Copyright © 2011 by Linda G. Hodge
All rights reserved. No part of this book may be reproduced by any mechanical, photographic, or electronic process, or in the form of a phonographic recording; nor may it be stored in a retrieval system, transmitted, or otherwise be copied for public or private use without written permission from the publisher.

ISBN: 978-09854107-2-8

Library of Congress Control Number: 2012937085

Edited by Penny Scott

Cover & Interior Design by Wendy Aguirre, Studio Wende Él, California

Author Photograph by Juan Roberts, CreativeLunacy

Scripture quotations marked (NLT) are taken from the Holy Bible, New Living Translation, copyright© 1996, 2004, 2007 by Tyndale House Foundation. Used by permission of Tyndale House Publishers, Inc., Carol Stream, Illinois 60188. All rights reserved.

Scripture quotations are from The Holy Bible, English Standard Version® (ESV®), copyright © 2001 by Crossway, a publishing ministry of Good News Publishers. Used by permission. All rights reserved.

Scripture quotations taken from the Amplified® Bible, Copyright © 1954, 1958, 1962, 1964, 1965, 1987 by
The Lockman Foundation Used by permission.
(www.Lockman.org)

For information regarding permission or additional copies, contact the publisher

KNOWLEDGE POWER BOOKS
A Division of Knowledge Power Communications, Inc.
Valencia, California 91355
661-513-0308
www.knowledgepowerbooks.com

Printed in the United States of America

This Book Belongs To

_____

Acknowledgements

Countless people are experiencing dreadful challenges, brought on by economic setbacks. Financial devastation has also created unusual trials to families, relationships and careers. Many are facing the tailspin of uncertainty, and are fearful of the future. This book is designed to ignite hope in a seemingly hopeless situation. With God's intervention, and caring others around us, we are able to pull ourselves out of the pit of despair.

I thank God for those who have assisted me in igniting this hope. Some have acted as a backdrop of determination and encouragement, while I have undertaken this project. It has been a wonderful journey working with those who have shared their stories. I'm confident such anecdotes behind these pages will also be a means of empowerment to you as well.

Eternal thanks to God who has gifted me with the ability to inspire and motivate through writing. I'm so forever grateful and never in a million years did I think this wonderful gift would be bestowed upon me.

This book shares heartfelt accounts of individuals who have taught me in special ways, what it means to bounce back from obstacles. Therefore, I give thanks to those individuals who allowed me to write their narratives and become transparent for readers like you. Their sorrows have not been wasted nor have they gone unnoticed.

Special thanks to my God-sent Editor, Penny Scott: for her collaboration and wordsmith skills that made the accounts even more relatable. Penny's expertise and coaching have inspired me and contributed to my love of "telling my story." You are the story behind the story.

I must give a Special "shout-out" to the ladies of Living Praise

Christian Center who have encouraged me along this journey, and supported me with words of affirmation and honor. You are truly the BEST!

Finally, I thank God for my deceased parents who made it all possible for me to live among the living for such a time as this. I know they must be blissfully proud of me, and cheering me on behind the "pearly gates of heaven." This book is yet another example of the faithfulness of God in my life: just another step of many more to come.

Table Of Contents

Words Of Encouragement 11

Introduction 15

1. Life's Obstacle Course 19

2. Fasten Your Seatbelt! 27

3. Don't Be Afraid to Stretch! 35

4. Wipeout 43

5. Survival of the Fittest 51

6. Uncommon Achievers 61

7. The Excuse Bag 71

8. The Football Game 81

Bibliography 99

Words Of Encouragement

Winning In Life: How to Bounce Back from Adversity, by Linda Hodge is a book that all should read. The revelation and reality of today's challenges, chaos, and confusion are presented throughout the chapters, with an unwavering assurance that God will be there to help you through. In these perilous (difficult) times, people are falling away and fainting due to insurmountable pressures and problems.

Linda Hodge has addressed so eloquently, yet without reservation – a word of hope that will help you to continue trusting in God's faithfulness. This is a book that must be read by those who are determined to walk in victory and fulfill their God given destiny. As you follow the principles outlined in this book, living victoriously and triumphantly in the midst of adversity is no longer an impossibility, but a certainty. As you awake to the challenges of life with resilience, readiness, and fortitude – you will always win. Linda's profound revelation of triumph in the midst of trials will set the wounded, weary, and wayward free. In her own life, Linda has displayed the strength and stamina to turn 'set backs' into a 'comeback.' The book is filled with examples of those who unwaveringly faced challenges and overcame them. You too are an over-comer, according to I John 5:4 – "For whatsoever is born of God overcometh the world: and this is the victory that overcometh the world, even our faith." God will reveal Himself through the pages of this book as the one who helps you overcome any and all obstacles.

In Linda's own words – "Setbacks are opportunities for comebacks." Setbacks and challenges are not the final word in your life, God's word is. God has established a covenant of hope with you. Genesis 6:18 "… I will establish my covenant with you". Allow God to fulfill His covenant in you. Steadfastly and firmly believe that success and victory is yours. Choose the winning life. Bounce back from adversity and allow your faith to be a witness to others that obstacles can't hold you back, but thrust you into a place of victory. Read this book, and learn how to fight with your faith. Win In Life – Bounce Back from Adversity!

*– **Dr. Jennifer Johnson***
Full Counsel Ministries Inc.
North Little Rock, Arkansas

It seems like we are living in an age where the Body of Christ needs to stop fighting to sit in the victim's seat. We must begin to put on the Full Armor of God so that we can withstand the unfair attacks and assignments that are strategically launched at us. In this book, Winning in Life: How to Bounce Back from Adversity, Pastor Linda Hodge gives profound insight on how to stop looking at our circumstances and embrace the mindset of Christ. Consider the mentality, "I can do all things through Christ which strengthens me." Refuse doubt, fear and bitterness, which hold the mind in bondage.

Each one of us have had unwarranted situations or disadvantages that have held us bound, discouraged, and feeling like a failure. But, we are not a people without hope! This is the church's finest hour so why then, are Christians stagnated, unproductive, and walking away from the vision God has given them?

Pastor Linda Hodge boils it down to one word, "disappointment." A few words that define disappointment are; frustration, unfulfilled, dissatisfaction, letdown, defeat and failure. These words play a pivotal role in our attitude.

If we are consumed with these emotions, it will show in our attitude, therefore, limiting us from accomplishing what we are called or desired to do. I believe this book is going to open our eyes and reignite a fire to the things we have quit, abandoned or never even attempted because of adversity. Anytime you try something greater than yourself, you are going to face challenges.

But Pastor Linda Hodge points out so eloquently, "It is there (during the course of life) that victory or defeat is determined over disappointments." No matter how the situation or circumstance appears, we must remove defeat from our minds and choose victory.

– Dr. Ginger Morgan
Harvest of Harmony International Church
Fresno, California

As I read Winning in Life: How to Bounce Back from Adversity, I thought of Judges 6. The story of Gideon where the angel of the Lord (Pastor Linda) spoke to Gideon (the readers) and the angel of the Lord had to build Gideon back up, because of the adversity and the pressures of life had beaten him down.

Sometimes we need to be reminded of the things that God has done for us and how God has brought us through; because we don't always keep our testimonies in front of us as David did when he confronted Goliath. He reminded himself of the Lion and the Bear and surely if God could deliver him from them he would deliver him from this uncircumcised Philistine.

Once you read this book you realize God can bring you through any and all situations because the battle has already been won but we must go thru to get to the finish line.

– Pastors Wilbur and Geri Ayers
Living Praise Christian Center
Chatsworth, California

Introduction

Have you ever considered your life as being one gigantic obstacle course? If you think about it, life has a way of offering numerous opportunities to maneuver your way from beginning to end: just like a challenge course. Contemplate, if you will, the intricate configurations of an obstacle course; endurance drills that test your physical stamina, coordination and psychological abilities. Such trials are designed to take you to an expected end in a timely manner. In other words, you aren't playing to lose, but to win.

Throughout each chapter, you will read about various challenges that come with just plain old living. Fortunately, there is always a strategy to winning any game. You will receive various victory-driven blueprints through a synergy of games, sports, and real-life triumphant stories. I cordially invite you onto the obstacle course of winning in life! All you need for this particular journey is an open mind and heart. Be prepared to view your tests from a totally different viewpoint – one that guarantees a comeback from a setback!

Bouncing Back from Adversity has been written specifically with you in mind: especially if you have been affected by the economic tailspin that we have been experiencing as a nation. Perhaps, you are recuperating from a horrendous relationship. Or, you've given up the fact that you might not ever be married. There are others who have experienced one of life's blows after the other! Auspiciously, many of you are working on putting your lives back together again! Whereby, some are in need of a few tools in overcoming challenges, setbacks and obstacles. Maybe, the tools are for you, some dear friend or family member. Whatever the case may be, it is no accident that you are holding this book in your hand.

You're closer than you think to bouncing back from obstacles and setbacks. Inside these pages, you will be enriched and empowered. However, you will also be stretched. I care about you so much that I couldn't leave you in your dilapidated state. There is a tremendous amount of potential in you waiting to be recognized. Sure, you may have been devastated, burned out, and in some cases, given up for dead or abandoned. Nevertheless, I have written this book to be a voice of hope and inspiration to you.

Bouncing Back from Adversity is packed with inspirational messages, and successful stories, that at one time looked to be completely hopeless situations. My objective is to encourage you to get your fight back. It's time to get back in the ring of life, and push back every obstacle that is trying to press against you. Each challenge comes to make you, not to break you. It's all in your response and your resolve to push through the difficult times. Seemingly impossible situations will either build you or defeat you; either you will overcome or be overcome.

You were born to dominate, and not be dominated under any circumstances. It's not time to retreat, but to advance. Things may have been delayed, but there's still no reason to quiver in the face of delay. Quitting is not an option for you. Your setback or challenge does not have the final word in your life, so STOP giving it a voice! As I survey my life, I have come to realize that God has not sent a storm my way to destroy me. But, He uses obstacles to grow, increase, and strengthen me!

"Now thanks be unto God, which always causeth us to triumph in Christ," (2 Corinthians 2:14).

The mere fact that God causes us to triumph means there is something to triumph over. When you have to triumph over something, it's usually a difficult ordeal. A triumph usually follows a period of hard fighting. At the end of the fight, one of the contenders eventually comes out victorious. You may be in a fight right now, but I have been assigned to ensure that you come out of the ring undefeated. Of course, you may encounter a few bruises and scars along the way. A few trips may have knocked you off-balance for a season. You see my friend, it takes determination to WIN! Nobody ever goes into the wrestling ring lightly. You must go with some ruthless determination to win. You must be, "victory-hungry," when you go into the ring; or else you will be carried out unconscious, embarrassed, and defeated.

My husband and I enjoy watching Ultimate Fighting Championship or "UFC®." In most instances, one of the contenders has more of a hungry look in his eyes than the other. At any rate, it takes more than wanting the win; one must have the skill, conditioning, strategy, concentration, and know his opponent's weaknesses. Conversely, you also must exhibit the same ambitious line of attack when planning to conquer your challenges in life. Throughout the pages of Bouncing Back from Adversity, you will receive the skills, mental and spiritual conditioning, as well as tactics and knowledge on how to recognize your opponent's game plan.

You will learn how to fight with your faith!

"Then he touched their eyes and said, 'According to your faith will it be done to you,'" (Matthew 9:29, NIV).

In this fight, your faith is in direct conflict with the enemy. The enemy knows that you are what your faith is. You will never get any victory that is bigger than your faith. You need faith for your victory. It has been completed; it is already done. But, you need to personally appropriate your faith to get into your victory. It is by walking with faith that you will overcome all difficulties and win your battles. Your victory is always guaranteed. However, you cannot live victoriously except you walk by faith.

"For whatever is born of God overcometh the world; and this is the victory that overcometh the world, even our faith," (I John 5:4). You are a winner.

You have a winner covenant with God, the Father.

He has destined you to win. You are not meant for failure and defeat, but for great exploits in victory. There is no fight, no battle that you can't overcome. Bad news may have been knocking at your door, but I have good news! The good news is that no matter what happens to us, God is faithful! And I declare, "No weapon that is formed against you will prosper!"

It's your Time to Bounce Back!

1
Life's Obstacle Course

A few years ago, I had the privilege of hosting a women's spiritual retreat. We set our sights on this wonderful campground, surrounded by flourishing green mountains and towering trees. Lush grass and lots of open space with easy walking trails made for enjoyable leisure and meditation times. Guests often cooled off at the center's Olympic-size swimming pool. Here, you could also find several outdoor eating areas offering stunning scenic views.

In fact, the ladies and I would meet at many of these picnic areas, and chat about the monumental moments we had experienced. However, this particular year, we decided to add a few surprises to our God-focused agenda. Why not think out-of-the box? We decided to explore more adventurous activities. Besides, the majority of us wanted to "just be girls for the day."

Thus, we packed our tennis shoes and some comfortable light clothing for this new journey. Wow! The planning committee had definitely designed an adventurous and rugged day of outdoor activities. We were paired off into groups of 10. And here is where the FUN began. Our mission commenced on a gigantic, football-size field with the sun beaming down upon us. We saw a myriad of obstacle courses. Looking around in bewilderment, we were all saying, "What have I gotten myself into?"

One challenge course consisted of the typical cloth sacks you would see at family gatherings. I ascertained there would be a few bumps and bruises coming from that exercise. But, it was the thought of "dashing" the 100- or-so yards down the field like an Olympic sprinter that made me and a lot of the other women nervous.

Of course, the planning committee tried reassuring us that we could accomplish any challenge. They even attempted consoling us in their motherly voice, "It's going to be fun, girls." Little did we know that the activities were spiritually-driven. The committee had transformed the huge football field into a full-blown obstacle course! The moral of the exercises were to teach us that we can overcome anything – provided we worked hard both individually, and as a team. Each participant was also supposed to contribute to the overall success of their challenge.

Our first test was the traditional sack race. Many of us were familiar with this game from our days in elementary school. Remember putting your legs in the sack, falling and tripping over the potato sack? Then, just too soon falling down once again? Well, one-by-one, we were placed in line to run down the field, as fast as possible. The finish line was approximately 100 yards down the field in view. Any team member who crossed the finish line first on the final stretch had the advantage of moving ahead on to the next obstacle course. Those few seconds or minutes give you a huge advantage over your opponent.

If you were not the "blessed" ones to have an advantage, then you had to make up time. We were brilliantly strategizing how we planned to rebound from lost time. Everyone wanted to stay in the game. When you think about it, that's really what life is all about. We all have opportunities presented to us due to obstacles, setbacks and disappointments. You can forge ahead and stay in the game of life, or give up and retreat. Some prefer to sit on the sidelines because they experience difficulty or challenge from an opposing force.

"Bouncing back" in life carries an intense determination to overcome challenges, delays and frustrations. There's an array of pain that has been served to you on a platter of defeat. In this particular chapter, we will deal with obstacles. Life's adversities are not prejudiced, nor are they exclusively for the weak and feeble. Unfortunately, hurdles are prescribed for every human being.

Ethnicity, creed, religion, environment, tradition, perception, self-esteem, or even the ability to love is a non-factor in life's adversities. Such factors are just part of life. There would not be life without some sort of adversity. Sadly, there is no mountain too high that you can hide from hardship. Nor, is there a valley too low that you can get under and avoid dealing with any type of hindrance.

Obstacles are considered stumbling blocks or barriers. During my years of driving, I have encountered various obstacles in the road. Some of the barriers were created by an object being in the middle of the road, while others were due to road constructions. At any rate, depending on the challenge, a mere maneuvering the car to the right or left was only warranted. Nevertheless, other deterrents caused me to completely have to exit the road and follow the detour sign.

> *Many times, obstacles have a way of bringing you face-to-face with yourself.*

On one particular evening, I was being oblivious to the direction the detour was taking me. I was familiar with the area and had a lot on my mind. Even worse, I was driving in foggy conditions. As the fog further impaired my vision, I found myself at the mercy of the detour signs!

Many times, obstacles have a way of bringing you face-to-face with yourself.

They identify your weaknesses and, at the same time, identify your strengths. This is exactly what happened when David encountered the giant, Goliath, in I Samuel 17. David, being only a shepherd boy, was the youngest of his brothers, the smallest in stature, and was the least candidate to overtake Goliath.

King Saul identified David's weakness, when in verse 33 he says, "You are not able to go against this Philistine to fight with him; for you are but a youth while he has been a warrior from his youth." There will always be a "King Saul" in life, who will tell you that you can't defeat a "Goliath". But David, who had become courageous, stouthearted and lionhearted through the obstacles he had conquered, began to vaunt to King Saul the victories that he had won.

> *It's especially important to get success under your belt!*

David purposely shared with King Saul his adventures with the lion and the bear that took a lamb from the flock; and what happened when he went after the animals. He attacked the lion and bear, and rescued the lamb from the lion's mouth. Not only did David rescue the lamb, but he killed the bear and lion. Because he fearlessly defeated that obstacle, David knew God would deliver him from the hand of the Philistine (Goliath).

It's especially important to get success under your belt! You've got to have some victories. It is winning that provides you with confidence. People who don't handle obstacles well are people who have histories of failure; they're afraid of obstacles. So exactly how do we successfully overcome an obstacle? There are three major steps to walking out victoriously.

First, you have to Count the Costs. David had to pay the price of criticism. When he charged his giant, he knew he was going to be criticized. I Samuel 17:28 reads:

> "Now Eliab his oldest brother heard when David spoke to the men; and Eliab's anger burned against David and he said, 'Why have you come down? And with whom have you left those few sheep in the wil-

derness? I know your insolence and the wickedness of your heart, for you have come down in order to see the battle."

In the process, you also have to learn how to handle toxic relationships. They can be people in the office, friends, or even family members. Toxic people are either skilled in poking holes or dampening your peace of mind. You feel drained energetically after a mere 10 minutes with them. Have you ever had to excuse yourself for a few minutes just to take a breather away from a critical person?

The moment you commit yourself to a project or goal, not only will your statements be tested, but others will express their doubts and tell you how to get it done. Oftentimes, the very person who can't handle the problem is more than willing to tell someone else how to handle it! Go figure that one!

Second, you must Charge Your Challenge. If you want to be effective in overcoming an obstacle, you have to get in the game and seize your chance to get into action. According to I Samuel 17:48-52, it continues:

> "Then it happened when the Philistine rose and came and drew near to meet David, that David ran quickly toward the battle line to meet the Philistine. And David put his hand into his bag and took from it a stone and flung it, and struck the Philistine on his forehead. And the stone sank into his forehead, so that he fell on his face to the ground. Thus David prevailed over the Philistine and killed him; but there was no sword in David's hand. Then David ran and stood over the Philistine and took his sword and drew it out of its sheath and killed him, and cut off his head with it. When the Philistines saw that their champion was dead, they fled. And the men of Israel and Judah arose and shouted and pursued the Philistines."

I consider that last verse to be the key to the whole story. This is the reason why we need to kill the giants in our lives and overcome obstacles. Those whom we lead or influence will never destroy the giants in their lives until we first kill the giants in our lives. When did the people shout? When did they charge? They did it after David had killed the giant. When you fail to conquer your own obstacles, the people who are following you will never become victorious. We have to face our obstacles head-on with purpose, precision, and perseverance.

Becoming victorious can be a daunting task. Very often, leviathans can make you feel like you are a joke. What you hold in your hand is insufficient. Consequently, you have to surprise them with quick, unexpected and precise moves. They are bullies, but they are slow because of their size. Remember: size is not always strength, but strength without strategy is futile. I Sam 17:41-44 continues:

> "Then the Philistine came on and approached David, with the shield-bearer in front of him. When the Philistine looked and saw David, he disdained him; for he was but a youth, and ruddy, with a handsome appearance. And the Philistine said to David, 'Am I a dog that you should come to me with sticks?' And the Philistine cursed David by his gods. The Philistine also said to David, 'Come to me, and I will give you your flesh to the birds of the sky and the beasts of the field."

But I love David's positive faith in response. He said in verses 45-47:

> "Then David said to the Philistine, 'You come to me with a sword, a spear, and javelin, but I come to you in the name of the Lord of Hosts, the God of the armies of Israel, whom you have taunted. This day the Lord will deliver you up into my hands, and

I will strike you down and remove your head from you. And I will give the dead bodies of the army of the Philistines this day to the birds of the sky and the wild beasts of the earth, that all the earth may know that there is a God in Israel, and that all this assembly may know that the Lord does not deliver by sword or by spear; for the battle is the Lord's and He will give you into our hands.'"

Countless people tell me, "Because you overcame your limitations and obstacles, I have the strength and courage to overcome mine." People look at me in amazement when I tell them how fearful and insecure I have been all my life. This journey of mine has not been easy, to say the least. I have learned: Conquer your fears then you can control your future.

In essence, insecurity has been a life-long battle. Now, keep that thought in mind. We will be addressing that in detail in a few upcoming chapters. Let's get back to this chapter. It is imperative for you to grasp this concept. A problem arises, when leaders are unwilling to confront their obstacles and giants. If they are not overcome, their followers will also be defeated and wallow in low self-esteem. When the leader fails, the people fail. When the leader fears, the people fear.

Third, you must Use Fear as Motivation to overcome your challenge. David realized the giant Goliath was a problem, but he also understood Goliath as an opportunity for promotion! Here's the difference between David and his brothers. His brothers looked at the obstacle and came to the conclusion Goliath was too big to hit. But David looked at the same obstacle and came to the conclusion it was too big to miss! Therefore, if you yield to obstacles, your ideas will die with you. Perception is extremely pivotal in every decision you make.

Every obstacle introduces a person to his own ideals. David wouldn't have realized his potential: the dormant ability that he possessed to do the impossible. It was imperative that he come in contact with Goliath. There are some people that come into your life only to shoot you like an arrow to your next destination. You thought they were there only to make your life miserable. Yet, they are not and were not positioned by accident. They have strategically been assigned to give you small successes, because small successes lead to greater successes.

Make everyday a victorious day over something, and build a track record of success.

Let each obstacle force you to go to the next level in God. No obstacle will ever leave you the way it found you. Consider this: every canned good you purchase at the supermarket has a life span printed on it. The lifespan varies from the consistency of the ingredients in the food. It was only designed to be edible during a certain period of time. The same goes for medication, which is manufactured only to be potent for a specified duration of time. Otherwise, after the expired time, it has no medical value to cause a cure in your body. Thankfully, every one of your obstacles has a limited lifespan. They are here only for a season: this too shall pass.

> *Make everyday a victorious day over something, and build a track record of success.*

So let's review. In order to overcome obstacles in your life, you must follow these steps:
1) Count the Costs
2) Charge Your Challenge
3) Use Your Fear as Motivation

I'm a witness that these steps do work. I have worked them time and time again in my life. My only question to you is, are you up for the challenge? Of course you are: if you weren't you wouldn't be reading this book. NOW read on...

2
Fasten Your Seatbelt!

An obstacle course is a series of difficult, physical barriers an individual or team must navigate, while often racing against a clock. Obstacle courses can include running, climbing, jumping, crawling and balancing elements with the aim of testing endurance. Occasionally, a course involves mental tests.

During the spiritual retreat, our team took a quick recovery from the previously exasperating challenge. We huddled up to encourage and inspire one another. Exhorting ourselves, we kept insisting that we could outlast our fatigue. By the way, our bodies were throbbing, and we were feeling total exhaustion. But, we mustered up the fortitude to get back on focus with our minds determined to stay in the game.

Some of the women were beginning to grumble about their legs feeling unstable due to the prior obstacle course. The 100-yard-dash pushed many close to the edge – and for good reason. Oh, boy! My body was not prepared for sprinting down the field! Running demands strenuous work on the hamstring and calf muscles. Surprisingly, we did have some ladies who exhibited the ability to bounce back due to their core strength. Our abdomen is considered our core, and a few participants experienced little pain during certain obstacle challenges. Core strength also causes you to maintain your equilibrium. If your core is strong, then you are less likely to experience injuries and it fortifies other areas of your body.

Let's take a sidebar for just a moment. We all have core values and beliefs that shape the way we view life's circumstances. Ultimately, this foundation affects how we react under pressure. Our beliefs programmed during childhood and adolescence created automatic, reactive attitudes and actions. Subsequently, those reactions helped in determining how we spontaneously respond to every aspect of our lives. Core values and beliefs have made us who we are today – both bad and good. So, what is holding you from bouncing back, or keeping you stuck; justifying your misery, lack, fear or dysfunction? I think I may be getting too deep. Time to get back on the obstacle course.

> *Setbacks are opportunities for comebacks!*

Well, although we were ready to forge ahead, we experienced a setback. Things had not gone the way we originally planned. We thoroughly calculated our strategy against our opponent. But, to our demise, some of our opponents had gotten the upper-hand. Fortunately, we knew this key factor.

Setbacks are opportunities for comebacks!

Many times, people count you out, too! They will tell you that you will never bounce back. You know those critics – they attach themselves to you like white on rice. Then, here you come: out of the ashes of overwhelming odds! You're back in the game!

We knew this setback was only a method to test our resilience: ability to rebound, our elasticity, and ability to recover. Our commitment to outlast our opposition would be our driving force to subdue our counterpart. Tenacity, which means determination, stamina, unshakable, uncompromising, strong-mindedness and firmness, was another link to overcome the obstacle course. Having a strategy is a must because it is the plan (blueprint). We could not win if we didn't have a scheme. It would not be accomplished through accidentally winning. The majority of the ladies were determined to win – they were no joke!

Mastering one's thoughts is crucial. How you see the problem, is the real problem. The greater the promise – the greater the problem. How you react during the problem determines how long you suffer from the problem. Paul exemplifies the qualities of perseverance. In 2 Corinthians 4:8-9 he says:

> "We are afflicted in every way, but not crushed; perplexed, but not despairing; persecuted, but not forsaken, struck down, but not destroyed."

Paul underwent shipwrecks, beatings, humiliation, and imprisonment. But, he came to understand that the difficulties that he endured were minuscule in comparison to the glory of God. Paul learned how to live on the other side of the coma. Our approach to handling problems in the past will greatly influence how we perceive them today.

> *The greater the promise – the greater the problem.*

A sculptor has a unique way of seeing things. I once heard that Michelangelo would walk around a block of marble for days; just walking around it, talking to himself. First, he would see (envision) objects in the rock. Then, he would go and chisel them.* It's really fascinating how a sculptor can visualize images that others can't see. He or she possesses this uncanny ability to picture what others can't see with the naked eye.

Often, a sculptor begins his work with a chunk of granite, a mallet and a chisel. Because of the artist's skill that he has acquired throughout the years, he is assigned an apprentice to help. The apprentice's training entitles him to thoroughly examine the master sculptor's work and follow along. In this way, the apprentice receives hands-on training. Many times, an apprentice is eager to speed up the process of sculpting his own art piece. He assumedly expects a clip of the rock to fall every time he hits the chisel with his mallet. To his surprise, he soon realizes nothing happens.

After a while, the apprentice lays down his mallet and chisel: he is feeling too discouraged to continue working. I can only imagine how the apprentice must feel by the end of a hard day. He thinks to himself, "Why can't I see the tangible results I was expecting?" The master sculptor, looking at him from afar, comes over to his apprentice and reassures him, "You must patiently take the mallet and tap the chisel." The veteran knows that a chip doesn't have to fall every time he strikes the chisel.

However, the master sculptor also realizes that every time he strikes the chisel, he's weakening the stone. If he remains patient and persistent long enough, the piece he wants to chip off will depart from the main rock. It's just a manner of time. Here's the moral of the story: You may be on the obstacle course of life and subjected to all sorts of setbacks. But if you would take what's in your hand, and skillfully navigate through your problems, then you will leap out of your troubles into a secure landing place.

> ***Problems are real, but never unsolvable.***

Problems are real, but never unsolvable. When you have a problem it means that it is only temporarily unsolvable to you. Temporarily is another term for the "time being." It's only for a brief or an allotted period. People are solving dilemmas and breaking world records in sports because they choose to leap out of the confinement of others' opinions, imprisonments and mindsets. On the other hand, some have never been told that they couldn't solve problems. Therefore, limitations were not a factor in their desire to finding solutions.

Problems must be clearly seen. If you can't clearly define the problem, you aren't able to conquer it. Some troubles need to be attacked systematically and not simultaneously. In any type of battle, the military force has been trained to strategically eliminate their opposition. This tactical plan to divide and conquer, little-by-little, gives them the advantage. And, if anything goes wrong, it allows them to make the necessary adjustments prior to their next attack. For example, if the armed forces must overtake five camps, then they would strategize by taking down the least resistant camps. After several victories, the military force moves toward seizing the most difficult enemy to overthrow. This approach gives the defense the confidence they need to dismantle the opposing force.

Problems are solved with help. Write a list of people and resources that can help you solve the problem. Oftentimes, it takes more than one person to work out a problem. Habitually, people try to solve their dilemmas by using their own limited resources instead of using the expertise of outside help. Through counseling countless people, I have come to learn that folks in general don't normally ask for help. I suppose the fear of what others will think about them keeps them from asking for assistance. We are a society that wants to be liked, not judged, criticized or slandered. Anything we feel that will sabotage our positive image we choose to hide and conceal.

Problems can stop you temporarily, but only you can stop yourself permanently. We can't continually handle problems in a way that is inconsistent with how we perceive ourselves. If we view ourselves as a person of worth, then we can begin to tackle big problems. Why? We are confident that we can handle anything that comes at us! You can tell whether you've growing emotionally and spiritually by the size of the problems that you're willing to tackle.

I believe anyone who does anything significant must first overcome the need of approval and acceptance of others. You simply cannot follow God and keep everyone happy all the time. Sure, you may have problems, but think about it. You may not be where you need to be, but thank God, you're not where you used to be! Every time I experience a mental relapse and take a mental trip back into my past, I begin to focus on my progress.

After all, life isn't about how fast I can reach my destination. Life is about how we make the trip to our destination. So choose to enjoy the process, knowing that your process is different from others. That kind of attitude infuriates the devil. Consider Hebrews 12:2-3 which says, "Looking away (from all that will distract) to Jesus, who is the leader and the source of our faith."

The devil is the author of distraction, and his intent is to cause your problems to become your destruction. God was not a bit surprised when you made the decision that altered your life. Psalm 139:1-4 states:

> "O Lord, thou hast searched me, and known me. Thou knowest my down sitting and mine uprising, thou understandest my thoughts afar off. Thou compass my path and my lying down, and art acquainted with all my ways. For there is not a word in my tongue, but lo, O LORD, thou knowest it altogether."

Every day of your life was written in His book before you ever showed up on planet earth. God knows every word that was ever spoken out of your mouth before it was spoken, and every word not yet spoken. Your problems do not shock Him.

Bad decisions don't change His unconditional love towards you. Unclean thoughts do not cause Him to take a double look at you. Your mistakes don't shame Him. Too many people treat their problems and failures as enemies. Instead, those situations should be considered opportunities for growth! There are little and big helpers that enter our lives to show us what and what not to do. Don't camp out with the problem and erect a monument to pay homage to the rest of your life! Don't make it a monument, but see it as a moment of time.

Don't scrutinize, analyze, and fantasize about your bad decisions or the problems you underwent in the past. Otherwise, you become paralyzed by the fear of making more bad decisions. You can't drive a parked car! Get going in some direction; if you make a wrong turn you can always go around the block and then head in the right direction.

On various occasions while traveling on an airplane, I recall hearing the pilot inform passengers that we were in a "holding" pattern. During this time, an airplane circles around a certain geographical area in the sky before it is cleared to land. This could last from five to ten minutes in duration. Throughout those times I thought, "Oh my God! I hope we have enough fuel." I have to shut my mind from seeing the plane falling from the sky as a result of an empty tank. OK, let's proceed back to the "holding" pattern; I just had a flashback.

In life, if we aren't careful, we will allow our problems to initiate our lives to be in a "holding" pattern. We will become like the children of Israel who wandered in the wilderness for 40 years, which should have only been an 11-day journey. Their past life of bondage and slavery had become so engrained in them that they couldn't see their way out of the wilderness. I believe the Israelites' fear of change caused them to be in confusion, and they weren't able to visualize the real problem. I'm sure they must have been between wanting change and fearing change.

To embrace any change, ask yourself the following questions, and in doing so, you are identifying the problem:

(1) What problems in my life am I currently experiencing because I'm resisting change?
(2) What it is costing me to keep things the way they are?
(3) What am I afraid of with respect to this change?
(4) What are the benefits if I make this change?
(5) What are the additional problems that can arise if I don't

make the change?

(6) When will I make the change?

When you decide to change and deal with the problem, you move your life into the next level of accomplishment. But, you must fasten your mental and spiritual seatbelts. Brace yourself for the turbulence; it may be a while before you reach that comfortable level again.

Nevertheless, you will reach comfort, but you must endure the turbulence of change in order to grow. I don't know what setbacks you are experiencing right now, but fasten your seatbelt. God is intentional, and His direction is strategic. He moves behind the scenes, orchestrating details and events in ways that can't be perceived by the human eye. Your problem will become your promotion!

> *Your problem will become your promotion!*

3
Don't Be Afraid to Stretch

In any game, I play to win – especially the game of life. I know to some that may sound rather strange; winning in the "game of life." Actually, when you really ponder about life, it is no more than a series of obstacle courses that each one of us must overcome and master. The mere existence of living carries an overwhelming sense of responsibility to us as well as others. Learning how to function in a dysfunctional society, and not taking into consideration the many limited options we have can be disheartening, to say the least.

My husband and I had the opportunity to travel abroad a few years ago. To our ultimate disbelief, we witnessed what we perceived as a severely disabled indigenous tribe of people. Interestingly, they were all traveling on scooters. The tribe did this not only as a means of transportation, but because they had no legs. Tribesmen used their hands to propel them down the foul, murky, and grimy paved streets. These diminutive and incapacitated bodies were traveling at high speeds to get to their destinations. What's more, they operated seemingly accustomed to their deprivation.

Of course, the tribe's nonfunctioning and inoperative bodies were quite a surprise to us. But as we observed from a distance, the people had learned to adapt to life despite not having legs. We concluded that the indigenous tribe's condition might have been preventable based on a couple of precepts. First, their circumstances would be a great deal healthier if the Third World country provided better nutrition, prenatal and medical care. Second, the hereditary defects might possibly have occurred in part because of the environment and numerous diseases that occupied the area in which they lived.

Consequently, the indigenous tribe contemplated another means of living a quality life with their limited options. Living life includes adjusting to disappointments along the obstacle course of life. Some things in life are like a "breeze" on a cool and sunny day. The wind silently passes through the leaves of a fully bloomed tree, while other trials may arrive in booming, thunderous sounds that shake everything around you, including yourself. Let's explore this a little deeper, I would like to invite you to take a walk with me in 2 Kings 7:3, 4:

> "...There were four leprous men at the entering in of the gate and they said one to another, 'why sit we here until we die? If we say, we will enter into the city, then the famine is in the city, and we shall die there: and if we sit still here, we die also. Now therefore come, and let us fall unto the host of the Syrians: if they save us alive, we shall live; and if they kill us, we shall but die."

Here were four lepers who were the least likely to succeed of anybody I have ever read. The word "disappointment" must have described them precisely without exaggeration.

A few words that define disappointment are: frustration, disillusionment, dissatisfaction, letdown, defeat, and failure. The lepers were highly unlikely candidates for success because they had three strikes against them. Number one, they suffered from leprosy. They were aware of the fact at some point this dreaded disease was going to kill them. Second, the lepers were starving to death. Enemy forces had come in and surrounded their city, cutting off its supply lines and causing a famine in the area.

Just imagine, not even the rich could purchase food because there was none to be found. And because of this disease, the leprous men were not allowed into the city gates to beg for whatever food was available. Third, the enemy was about to attack and destroy everyone. Our modern day vernacular would say, "They were thrown under the bus." Thus, these four men did not face a very promising and secure future. If their leprosy didn't kill them, then they would die of starvation: provided the enemy didn't come and kill them with their swords first.

Now pay attention-if anyone had a right to feel disappointed, have a bad attitude, and feel pathetic, it was these sickly guys. No one will argue that fact at all. In the natural, the lepers had nothing to live or hope for; and nothing to motivate, inspire or encourage them. You and I think we have problems because our light bill is due, or we're late on our house mortgage or our car note. We think we're stressed out because we have overextended ourselves in our excessive, self-gratification spending habits.

Now, I am not belittling or demeaning your situation. But surely it can't be as desperate or as devastating as the situation in which these men found themselves. But, as we will see, something happened to change the lepers' situation. And it happened when they had a change of attitude.

"Why sit we here until we die?," they asked themselves. That was a thought-provoking question. It stirred up expectation and ignited in them zeal to at least try something.

Instead of sitting and waiting to die, they decided to do something: they took action.

Their attitude was, "If death is coming for us, then it is going to have to get us on the move because we aren't going to just sit here and passively wait for our demise. We are going to get up and go to the camp of the enemy. If they let us live, that is fine. But, if they kill us, at least we would have put forth an effort."

Those sickly men chose to go into action: instead of sitting there in misery and despair, consumed with disappointment, complaining and crying. They stood to their feet, not only physically but mentally. The lepers set themselves into motion. Don't be like the majority who choose to take the least resistant approach. Untie your feet, remove yourself from a defeated position and enter the battle. The combat zone is in the mind. The battle is waged while we are about life, going about our daily routine. It is there (during the course of life) that the victory or defeat is determined over disappointments. Consider how the lepers went into battle. 2 Kings 7:5-9 states:

> "And they rose up in the twilight, to go unto the camp of the Syrians: and when they were come to the uttermost part of the camp of Syria, behold, there was no man there.
>
> For the Lord had made the host of the Syrians to hear a noise of chariots, and a noise of horses, even the noise of a great host: and they said one to another, Lo, the king of Israel hath hired against us the kings of the Hittites, and the kings of the Egyptians, to come upon us.
>
> Wherefore they arose and fled in the twilight, and left their tents, and their horses, and their asses, even the camp as it was, and fled for their life.
>
> And when these lepers came to the uttermost part of the camp, they went into one tent, and did eat and drink, and carried thence silver, and gold, and raiment, and went and hid it; and came again, and entered into another tent, and carried thence also, and went and hid it.
>
> Then they said to one another, we do not well: this day is a day of good tidings, and we hold our peace:

if we tarry till the morning light, some mischief will come upon us: now therefore come that we may go and tell the king's household."

I'm convinced that as soon as these four lepers began to walk toward the enemy's camp, the Lord caused their footsteps to be magnified. They sounded like the marching tread of a mighty army. The clamorous, piercing, earsplitting sound must have been what the Syrian soldiers heard as they sat in their camp with plenty to eat and drink, while waiting for the people of Israel to die of starvation and deprivation.

> *Here was a no-win situation that God turned into a triumph!*

Nevertheless, God intervened and the Syrians heard the sound of chariots and horses and thousands of disciplined troops. As a result, they were so frightened, they didn't even send out a scout to see the size or strength of the approaching army. Instead, the Syrians leaped to their feet and fled in utter terror, leaving behind all their food, drink, gold, silver, clothing and weapons of war! Wow!

Here was a no-win situation that God turned into a triumph! I believe that God is ready to do the same in our circumstances. All He is waiting for is us to get up, brush ourselves off, and to boldly declare, "Satan, I am not sitting here until I die! I am not going to accept disappointment and defeat as a way of life. I am going into action! And I will be victorious!"

Instead of sitting and waiting to die, they decided to do something-to take action. Yes, it may be a fact that you are outwardly losing ground on the obstacle course of life. Perhaps, you are in combat. You must climb over a few disappointments, crawl under some difficult decisions, and balance yourself for the battle. Maybe, you need to jump over some puddles of muddy water in order to swing across some ropes and nets. Dealing with disappointments will require you to make adjustments. Wrong attitudes must be discarded.

You will be required to stretch in ways you never knew were possible. Most people are vulnerable when they are stretching. When a rubber band is pulled tight, it's much easier to break. A runner who's stretching to cross the victory line is in a precarious position. If you were to push him a little bit, you could knock him clear off his course. Every energy, every muscle, every fiber, is aiming toward a goal: leaving the runner vulnerable.

Such is the exact situation that occurred this past summer when my 10-year-old grandson, Ezekial, was running at the 2011 AAU Junior Olympic Games held in New Orleans, Louisiana. He entered the race ranked second nationally in the 800-meters event. Ezekial took home the gold medal the previous year. As the race began, it was a tough squeeze for him trying to gain position toward the inside lanes. This is a spot most distance runners prefer as the turns are shorter, and it places you at an advantage when running the sprints on the straight part of the track.

> *You will be required to stretch in ways you never knew were possible.*

Ezekial had about 200 meters left before he could claim another victory. He knew he had the speed to overtake the other runners around the corner and down the stretch. Unfortunately, while he and his teammate were both aiming toward an inside lane, they collided on the track. Both boys lost their balance. However, that was not the end of Ezekial's race. He waited until everyone ran over and around him. Then, he got up to speed past other runners. He wasn't able to retain his gold medal, but he did settle for an 8th place medal out of 16 runners in the competition. Considering the year before he brought home the gold trophy, of course Ezekial was disappointed not medaling in the top three places.

Two days later, Ezekial and his teammates were back on the track. It was Ezekial's last chance to compete for a gold medal.

This time, Ezekial's team was running in the 4-by-800 meters relay championship. Ezekial was set to run the anchor leg. Well, the proud "Nana" that I am, I must report to you that they won the gold medal! Now, Ezekial could have allowed disappointment to overtake him. Instead, he took a different approach. He allowed the pain of earning 8th place in the previous competition to stretch him. Ezekial successfully ran anchor for the team and was instrumental in sprinting ahead of the others and winning the gold!

Most people begin their lives by stretching, and they soon discover that this position leaves them susceptible to attack and criticism. They start to equate stretching with pain. Some choose to opt out of the game of life, and are not willing to stretch any longer. Every fitness coach or trainer will tell you that it is important to stretch your muscles prior to and during any exercise routine. This allows the muscles to warm-up and decreases the probability of injury.

During those disappointing seasons in your life, you have to take a minute to stretch yourself. Amidst these stretching moments, which sometimes seem to be an eternity, we are vulnerable to the reactions of others. Sometimes, we can be helpless to ourselves. We are often harder on ourselves than other people. Consequently, we can't allow that to become a deterrent for stretching ourselves to success. Sure we will fail from time to time, but we must learn how to deal with it. Don't ever let failure become final!

Everyone needs a few cheerleaders; the best way to pull out of disappointment and discouragement is to surround yourself with people who will encourage you. Make sure you enlist a few cheerleaders in your life.

Now back to our biblical story. Here's the irony of this situation: the mighty army of the Syrians did just what the four poor Israeli lepers refused to do; they gave up without a fight. As a result, they lost everything. And the lepers won everything. The battle was decided in the mind of these four, "hopeless and homeless," outcasts. The first step to victory is a changed attitude. So, here's my question to you. What does this story of the four lepers say to us today? It says that in the mind of God, we are triumphant, and not defeated. If we will have the courage to rise up and step forth in the march of faith, we can win on the obstacle course of life.

> ***If we will have the courage to rise up and step forth in the march of faith, we can win on the obstacle course of life***

4
Wipeout

The reality game show *Wipeout* on the ABC/Disney network revolves around the objective of completing water-based obstacle courses. Contestants are required to complete obstacles that must be navigated sequentially. The tests are a rigorous challenge of total body fitness and high intensity, cardiovascular capacity. In order for the contestant to move on to the next challenging test, they must first pass the previous obstacle challenge. The remaining final contestants have successfully secured their position through enduring strenuous obstacles, as well as having completed the task in the least amount of time.

The winner is then awarded a monetary gift as a result of his accomplishment. Winning in life may not promise monetary gifts, but it does guarantee a fulfillment of accomplishment and a sense of empowerment. Sometimes, victories can only be achieved through tremulous seasons of our lives. And, when we are traveling through the rough terrains of life, endurance must be enforced. This type of fortitude is associated with the physical stamina required for a race. However, the character quality of endurance is much deeper than physical stamina. It includes the strength to tolerate under pressure.

To endure is to tenaciously hold on until a goal is accomplished. Jacob clung to the angel and declared, "I will not let you go until you bless me!" God not only blessed him but affirmed, "Thy name shall be called no more Jacob, but Israel: for as a prince hast thou power with God and with men, and hast prevailed," (Genesis 32:28).

Endurance is based on hope. It is focusing on a goal greater than the distractions along life's way. A runner will endure rigorous and painful training in hope that he will win the race. He performs arduous drills, body strengthening and circuit training routines just to get the edge on his opponent.

> *Endurance is based on hope.*

He is aware that champions are the ones that set the pace for winning the race. Victors only need minuet seconds to win a race. Therefore, every strive they take can cause them to win or lose the race. Two fears of a runner are; running out of strength before reaching the goal, and reaching the finish line without energy left.

> "And let us not be weary in well-doing: for in due season we shall reap, if we faint not," Galatians 6:9.

> Speaking of the power of endurance let me introduce you to a young man named Justin. He was born deaf, and by all accounts was considered disabled and disadvantaged. Oddly, it wasn't until Justin was 2-years-old, that his parents were told by doctors that he was deaf. Leaving the office in ultimate desperation, his parents could not fathom the fact that their first-born child was deaf. The son they had anticipated would bring so much joy, and whom they had many hopes for, wouldn't be able to live a "normal life."

I sat on the couch speaking to his mother, Jackie, as she recounted in her mind the awful and horrifying day, as if it was just yesterday. The memory I noticed was both distasteful and comforting at the same time. The joy of his success somewhat out-weighed the pain of the past. However, she lived with the fear of him not being able to "cope" until his first day of school. Justin exhibited the typical eagerness and boisterous behavior of a 6-year-old boy ready to embark upon his whole new world of independence. And Jackie says she experienced, "calmness and overwhelming joy," as she walked away from his classroom. Now looking back, she says she felt that Justin would be OK.

Consequently, she recalls having to, "set a few teachers straight." Jackie says she told them, "There is nothing wrong with Justin other than the fact that he is deaf." Physically, emotionally, and intellectually he was just like any other young boy his age. With his athleticism and determination not to be different than any other boy, Justin wanted to try out baseball in Little League at 5-years-old. Although there was much reservation from Little League advisors, greater support came from Derek, Justin's dad. The determined little boy was allowed to play.

Derek assembled a team of both deaf and hearing players. Justin's outstanding athletic abilities surprised both his parents, as well as the Little League association. His courage and no-quit attitude inspired him to play additional sports; track, basketball and football. Moreover, the fearless composure that he exhibited gave Justin the fortitude to attend mainstream schools, instead of hearing-impaired schools. Participating in all the "normalcy" of school activities as his peers boosted his confidence even more.

As we fast forward into Justin's life after the commencement of high school, it brings me pleasure to report that he continues to be living the "normal" life of a young man. He is now working and tutoring other deaf students while attending Rochester Institute of Technology. Justin recently completed his Associate of Arts Degree in Accounting and is enrolled in his third year of college. He is pursuing a Bachelor's of Arts degree in Marketing. Justin's goal is to eventually take over the family's accounting business, and provide services for the deaf community. Presently, he has the opportunity to study abroad for the summer, and experience other countries. As his mother and I came to the close of our conversation, the last words she expressed to me were empowering.

Jackie says, "His father and I never put limits on him. Therefore, he never put limits on himself."

The difficulty of living in a world whereby communication is such a key in forging ahead to reach your destiny is vital and crucial. The art of communication is one of the most powerful elements in expressing yourself, as well as relating to others. Relationships hinge on the ability to communicate and articulate your aspirations and dreams.

Many times, the capacity to verbalize your thoughts and ideas affords you an extraordinary advantage over your peers.

Society places much demand on the usage of words, as well as the articulation of how you use your words. With all of the societal demands on communication, it is awe-inspiring how one who is deaf has a chance of thriving in a communicative society!

Justin's story is unique in the sense that his disability has not disabled him from living a fully productive life. As a matter of fact, he has learned to navigate through life despite his hearing obstacles. I asked Justin if he wouldn't mind sharing with us his thoughts on what motivates him and makes him determined to win in life. This is what he had to say:

> "I have learned how to have the right response to my situations. I refused to blame others for my circumstances. I determined that I wouldn't feel sorry for myself. This is a trap that accomplishes nothing positive. I choose not to escape the problem, but instead activate, 'spiritual faith muscles.'"

Although Justin is living thousands of miles away from home, he has refused to allow the conventional method of communicating by telephone to become a stumbling block. Instead, he is using what is in his hands and his fingers (advanced texting and emailing) as his "voice" of communication. End of Story!

What is in your hands that you aren't using as a tool to overcome your obstacles in life? Of course, we cannot change some things. Sure, we can't change the color of our skin. However, there are some that make the attempt. We cannot change a hurtful past. What we can do is change how the past affects us. We cannot change how others see us. They have already come to their conclusion. What we can change is how we see ourselves. The past has already been written.

> *We have the power to write our future with our mouth, based on the Word of God, and based on who we are and what we do now.*

We have the power to write our future with our mouth, based on the Word of God, and based on who we are and what we do now.

God's Word says he has an expected end for us. Therefore, I choose to live life with purpose, and with a mission. Jesus made it clear; difficulties are to be expected. He told His followers in John 16:33, "These things I have spoken to you, that in me you may have peace. In the world you have tribulation, but take courage; I have overcome the world." Because we are in Him, we can expect a glorious outcome over every situation.

Some of you reading this book are facing extreme difficulties in your life and can't see your way. But I want you to know that I see a bright future for you just ahead.

Wintertime driving conditions in Texas aren't favorable. I would often experience early morning fog. Clouds can be so thick short distances ahead can hardly be seen. On certain days, when driving to my destination, my vision was almost dangerously impaired. Although driving slowly with my high beams on, the mere fact of not knowing what lay ahead was dreadfully frightening. If truth be told, the mere thought of not being able to see almost put me in a state of paranoia. Like other drivers on the road, I too, was perturbed by the hazardous conditions.

There were numerous occasions where my first indication was to turn the car around and return home. Thoughts would race in my mind a mile a minute, "Why don't I just turn this car around, and go back home?" But I had a destination to reach. Besides, others were counting on me to be on post for my job. So, I reluctantly put the pedal to the metal, doubled-checked that my seatbelt was fastened, adjusted my attitude, and drove down the dark, foggy road. Still, the fog of confusion was seemingly suffocating me from all sides. Yet, I remained unwavering that I could focus my attention on staying on the road towards my destination.

One of the focal points that enabled me to drive on the road was the front car's headlights. As long as the headlights were in front of me, I felt a sense of security and assurance. It provided me the ability to see just beyond where I was driving, even though I could only see a couple of hundred feet ahead. Conversely, the light of God's Word has the ability to direct you through your desert experiences. According to Psalm 19:7-8:

> "The law of the LORD is perfect, reviving the soul. The statutes of the LORD are trustworthy, making wise the simple. The precepts of the LORD are right giving joy to the heart. The commands of the LORD are radiant giving light to the eyes."

Paul says in Philippians 1:18, "What then? Notwithstanding, every way, whether in pretence, or in truth, Christ is preached; and I therefore do rejoice, yea, and will rejoice." From the example of his life, the Apostle Paul expected God to turn every negative situation into a positive one. He fully expected every crisis to be transformed into a triumph. Although locked up in prison, Paul writes to the church in Philippi, encouraging them to take heart and not to be misled by appearances. The Apostle Paul explains to them that, despite the way his circumstances may be viewed, he fully expects it to turn out for his good.

In verse 18 of Philippians 1 Paul says in essence, "I intend to rejoice over what is happening here and to continue to rejoice." I believe Paul knew that if he kept his attitude right, he would prevail over his temporary setback.

If you will keep your attitude right, then you, too, will prevail over your obstacles.

I don't know who I'm talking to right now, but get this: "You will prevail!" According to your earnest expectation and your hope, says Philippians 1:20, we receive in direct proportion to what we expect. I will be the first to admit that I seldom know how God is going to fulfill His Word. But I do know that He is going to fulfill it. That's why, having done all, I stand according to Ephesians 6:13:

> *If you will keep your attitude right, then you, too, will prevail over your obstacles.*

"But how long do you stand?"

That's simple. I stand until I win.

"How long does it take to win?"

Until you don't have to stand anymore.

What am I saying? I am saying that when we take a stand of faith, there is no compromising, backing off, giving up, giving out, or giving in. I hope you are up for the challenge of winning in life.

Here are a few things you must do in order to stand and win;

1. Admit that God, not man, is your source.
2. Don't panic.
3. Don't limit God.
4. Trust God to vindicate you.
5. Act on principle, not feelings.

Paul was a veteran of adversity. Life after his conversion to Christ was one calamity after another; beatings, shipwreck, stoning, and imprisonment, to name a few of adverse adventures. Yet, the world has never forgotten him. WHY? The Apostle Paul chose to CONQUER and not be conquered.

"Nay, in all these things we are more than conquerors through him that loved us," Romans 8:35. Champions think differently. They refuse to waste their energy and thoughts on their obstacles.

Champions concentrate on their goals.

Whatever adversity you are wrestling with today or tomorrow, you can be assured that you are never isolated from the love of God. Never give up during your adversity!

Give in to Christ and His love for you. You will find yourself advancing through each and every hardship; moving from strength-to-strength. Consider Lamentations 3: 21-23:

> "This I recall to my mind, therefore I have hope. The Lord's loving kindness indeed never ceases, for His compassions never fails. They are new every morning; great is Thy faithfulness."

5
Survival Of The Fittest

Surfing TV channels is a luxury that doesn't always afford me the opportunity to explore as I would desire. But, one evening while relaxing, I indeed found myself complementing on what I wanted to watch, while unwinding after a hectic day. I discovered a fascinating reality show called Survivor. It is an unscripted television program produced in numerous countries throughout the world. The show uses a system of progressive elimination tests, allowing contestants to vote off other tribe members until only one final contestant remains and wins the title of "Sole Survivor."

During the course of the game, players compete as tribes or individually in contests. Challenges consist of endurance, strength, agility, problem-solving, teamwork, dexterity, and/or willpower. The degree of difficulty may be progressively increased during the course of an endurance challenge in order to arrive at a winner faster. A player chosen as Sole Survivor receives a cash prize of one million dollars. Now, that's a reason to survive! I'm sure if more of us were rewarded a monetary gift for surviving; we would have a whole boatload of survivors at the loading dock.

Winning certain challenges offers several advantages for individuals as well as tribes. For example, contestants are afforded the opportunity to receive "immunity," which simply comes as the result of winning a particular game challenge. This is a huge advantage, because under no circumstances can they be voted off the show at that particular time. Therefore, it brings the contestant one step closer to winning the grand prize. Unfortunately, in "real-life" there is no such thing as immunity to help us become survivors on this journey of life.

Jesus, Himself, suffered an unimaginable death despite having exemplified a flawless life. And so, who we are to think we may skip past adversity? It just won't happen. No amount of man's interpretation of goodness will ever qualify him or exempt him from a few or many setbacks in life. Jesus reminded His disciples and us in John 16:33, "In this world you will have trouble." But that's not the end of the story. He said, "Be of good cheer, for I have overcome the world." He didn't promise a shielded life: that's free of heartache and pain. As a result, many of us who are faithful Disciples of Christ stand at the edge of bad news, from time to time.

Such was the case of Angela when she was informed by her obstetrician that her beautiful, unborn baby girl had a choleductal cyst growing on her gall bladder. If left untreated, this condition could be cancerous for the infant. You too, also may have received some bad news that you feel has knocked the "breath of life" out of your wings. But, I'm here to resuscitate you with the Word of God. So, on the count of three, I want you to breathe again. Ready, set, let's count aloud.

> *Life isn't over! It's time to breathe in the strength of God.*

One, two, three! "Breathe!" Life isn't over! It's time to breathe in the strength of God. The Bible says, "In my weakness, He is made strong." He rescues, redeems and heals. Just hold on my friend!

As Angela drove away from the doctor's office on that dreaded day, she wasn't alone in the front seat of her car. Fear was sitting next to her. Somehow, it had managed to get in the car without her knowledge. Yet, begging her to give him her full attention. Within a matter of moments, Angela soon realized fright's presence. His taunting words of hopelessness and terror soon engulfed the car, like a dark cloud of despair. A grim ray of hope was lurking like the sun diminishing on any given afternoon. It was then that Angela felt an uninvited passenger had hitch-hiked a ride. Angela was well familiar with fear's presence. But, she was determined to know her God more. Angela's past triumphs in life over insurmountable odds was the driving force that beckoned this faithful woman to remain calm.

She was determined to do it under a seemingly unbearable situation. Angela's unborn daughter was already experiencing an overwhelming setback. Nevertheless, Angela pulled herself together. Feelings of terror and defeat began to roll away like a dark cloud on a warm, sunny day. She knew that by faith she was up for the challenge.

So, on August 30, Ananda was born weighing barely five pounds. She was immediately sifted out the arms of Angela and into Neonatal Intensive Care Unit for evaluation and testing. The cyst was rapidly growing on Ananda's gall bladder. Little did Angela know the incomprehensible road that was awaiting her and little Ananda. For eight ragged months she anticipated the day until Ananda was big enough to sustain the ordeal of removing the cyst through surgery. Ananda's surgeon feared operating sooner would possibly be more life-threatening. At the same time, Ananda was experiencing extreme acid reflux attacks that blocked her airways, causing the infant to be rushed to the nearest hospital Emergency Room on several occasions for respiratory distress.

One medical condition turned into multiple with Ananda now requiring a gastric specialist to oversee acid reflux issues that were starting to damage her esophagus. It was discovered that Ananda was severely allergic to both breast milk and the soy milk formula she was being fed. Once the formula was changed to the highest hypoallergenic type, the reflux issues calmed. However, Ananda's gastric specialist recommended surgery on Ananda's esophagus if her acid reflux issues didn't clear up. Unfortunately, despite those health issues, the surgery clock continued on the gall bladder. "It was agonizing as the wait of eight months lingered on," Angela recalls. She says, "It felt like a lifetime. All of these small battles came along while I waited for the big war."

Many times, waiting can be a strenuous ordeal. Our emotions escalate like a playground swing seat. One moment we are up in the sky, and the next moment we are being carried from off the ground. If we give our emotions the luxury to rule our lives, we will unfortunately be living from day-to-day, depending on our minute-to-minute sensitive swings. On an emotional level, if we have to contact our moods on whether we are having a good productive day, then we are giving feelings control over us. But thankfully we can make a decision that we won't allow our circumstances to dictate how we feel.

We can have victory rather than live a life subjected to a victimized mentality. This person exists from a disadvantaged position and dwells like a slave, rather than a victor in life. Daily, we are all confronted with mood swings, choices and decisions that we must choose to make. Each day, we must decide not to live on the defensive: and no longer wave a white flag of surrender and defeat. Instead, we are pressing the battle: going to wage offensive war to win.

> *We can have victory rather than live a life subjected to a victimized mentality.*

"We are troubled on every side, yet not distressed; we are perplexed, but not in despair. Persecuted, but not forsaken; cast down, but not destroyed," 2 Corinthians 4:8-9.

Through Christ you are restored to full control of your emotions, and the ability to bring every thought under the power of the Holy Spirit gives you the advantage.

This is what Angela had to do on a daily basis while waiting for Ananda's surgery to take place. She wrestled with images of losing her infant on the operation table. Inside your mind, images are created. This secluded "room" of your mind is where images are incubated. These images either present victory or defeat; this is where the mental warfare begins. The moment those negative defeating thoughts and imaginations begin to invade our minds, we must use the power of our restored will to resist them, and cast them down in the Name of Jesus! We must, "bring every thought unto captivity." This is where the real victory is won!

Eight months had finally arrived for Ananda's surgery. Angela awakened that early morning to feelings of turmoil and relief simultaneously. Contemplating, and wondering if her baby would be OK, while concurrently feeling the peace of God. She was filled with a bottle of mixed emotions and trembling. Yet, she was also trusting as she inhaled in and exhaled out. Reiterating to herself, as if she was trying to convince herself, all is well. Angela was rehearsing in her mind, "Blessed be the God and Father of our Lord Jesus Christ, the Father of mercies and God of all comfort," (2 Corinthians 1:3, NASB). This verse, was like a "miracle pill" that she kept consuming as she traveled from her home to the long awaited Children's Hospital, where a team of doctors and nurses had assembled to prep little Ananda and begin the surgery.

Her faith in God was at its ultimate test. Everything that she had believed in all her Christian life was at the earmark of being tried. Angela had entered into a divine moment of time; it was her and her God. Today, she would fully come to know JEHOVAH-NISSI, "The Lord is Conqueror." This Name reveals God as a mighty deliverer or conqueror who always defeats the enemies of His people. She had learned early on in her Christian life that Jesus had conquered our enemy, and stripped him of his power; destroyed the power of sin, sickness and death. That same power was Ananda's passport and guarantee to victory!

Sitting in that waiting room, she came to realize that God was EL-SHADDAI, "The Almighty God." That name reveals His all-sufficient and almighty power that is the supreme power over all. The word "shaddai" in Hebrew refers to a woman's breast. This expresses God's desire for His people to draw sustenance and strength from Him as a child is fed and nourished at its mother's breasts. And oh! How she needed the supernatural strength that only God can give. On that particular day, Angela came to know her God as, JEHOVAH-RAPHA, "The Lord is Healer." She rehearsed in her mind of all the stories that Jesus had healed people throughout the Bible, as He went from village to village healing all manner of diseases. As He opened blind eyes, restored hearing, made the lame to walk, and healed all who were oppressed of the devil. "Surely," she said within herself, "This is a little job for him to do."

The four-hour scheduled surgery had turned into six hours of agonizing anticipation in waiting for the physicians to give her the outcome of the surgery. Staring at the door to open, and hoping her "hospital pager" would ring at any moment had become frustrating and draining, to say the least. Finally, after six hours, the doors swung open, accompanied with a look of relief and a big smile on the head surgeon's face, that lit up the whole room. The surgery was a success! They had safely removed the golf ball-size cyst along with Ananda's gall-bladder, and a portion of her intestines. And, within five days, Ananda was sent home with a clean bill of health.

Little did Angela know at the time, that two months later Ananda would be hospitalized again. Due to complications of her previous surgery, Ananda contracted C-Difficile (the Super bug). She battled back-to-back bouts of enteritis after her gall bladder and intestines were removed. Here again, Angela's faith was being tested. Wondering how could this be possibly happening? But again, Angela set her trust in God. Paul says that he "set" his hope on God. The word, "set," means to position something. Angela made a deliberate and conscious decision to put her hope completely in the Lord. You and I have to make the same intentional choice. We must remember where to look.

But this is not the end of the story. As a result of Ananda's complications, she was hospitalized at Children's Hospital in the Pediatric Intensive Care Unit for 25 days. And, 19 of those days she was hooked to a ventilator with a tracheotomy. Ananda even suffered through a bout of pneumonia. "What an ordeal!" Angela sighed with relief as she finished telling me the story. Looking at her now bubbly 4-year-old daughter, one can see that she is thriving just as any "typical" 4-year-old. By the way, she is one of my favorite little people.

Today, I want you to know that God is your comforter.

Whatever has come to trouble your spirit, whatever physical challenges you may face, despite the choices one of your children has made, or the uncertain financial future you face; wherever your soul trembles, call on our God, who makes a promise to be true to his character. He gives comfort in all our troubles.

As a 1-year-old toddler who is taking first steps must feel survival mode: merely taking one step at a time. I can imagine them thinking, "If I can get a few steps in without falling on the floor, Mommy would be so proud of me." Consequently, after a number of years, one learns that first baby steps are only a picture of what is to come in surviving the real world. Living life has a way of bringing an undeserved measure of challenges and obstacles that one must master in order to survive the real world.

Through the power of the Holy Spirit living within us we have the ability to tear down every barrier of negativity and unbelief that attempts to come our way, in challenging times.

It was this power that later transformed the disciples into fearless men and women who were full of faith and courage. They were willing to lay down their lives rather than deny the Lord. It's through faith and by the Word of God that we must realign our thinking. God's Word says, "I can do all things through Christ who strengthen me," Philippians 4:13. By faith, in the Word, Jesus defeated Satan in the wilderness. By faith, He performed miracles. By faith, He committed Himself into the hands of God in the Garden of Gethsemane. By faith, He endured the agony of the cross. By faith, He defeated Satan. He was raised triumphant over Satan and all his evil principalities and powers. He is now seated in a position of supreme power and authority at the right hand of the Father!

Friend, the war has been won. Jesus has overcome the world! In Him you, too, have won because He has become the author and the source of your faith. Know this, not only is Jesus the author of our faith, He is the "Perfector" of our faith. The Greek word used for "perfecto" of our faith means, "to bring to maturity; to become full-grown." Your victory over your situation and circumstance is not dependent upon a faith you can somehow produce. It is dependent upon Christ's faith that is in you. Jesus has placed His faith in you, and it is He who will cause your faith to increase. So believe me, as you continue to exercise the faith He has given you concerning His promises: He will strengthen your faith and cause it to grow and develop until it is perfected and brought to full maturity.

> *Faith is like film: it develops in the dark.*

Faith is like film: it develops in the dark.

When you enter a room with the lights off, you walk into all sorts of things. You are surprised and sometimes, physically hurt because you didn't realize what was in front of you. But when the light switch is turned on, you can suddenly recognize and see your surroundings. When you operate in the "light" of faith and in His Word, you are able to handle any type of obstacle or temporary setback. You can "see" the blessings that are in front of and all around you.

The power of the Word and faith cannot be minimized; it is the way to see the light at the end of the tunnel! Therefore, when you are in a situation and you cannot see a way out, you have to allow the Word to shine the light on your mind; so you won't be overwhelmed.

"The entrance of thy Word giveth light; it giveth understanding unto the simple," Psalm 119:130.

When the Word of God enters you, it produces a miracle light, and you become a master in that area of your life.

When the Word of victory enters you, transformation takes place and you become a victor. When the Word of holiness enters you, becoming holy ceases being a struggle. This is the same in every area of your life. My husband and I have had to walk through many challenges and many obstacles. Many times, while trusting and trembling simultaneously. Every time the enemy would try to discourage us, we would declare the faithfulness of God! The light of the gospel of Jesus Christ washed out all the attacks of the enemy against our mind. God has proven Himself to us over and over again.

There is only one thing that is going to help you stand while everything around you is being shaken; the Infallible, Impregnable Word of God. Regardless of the circumstances that have come into your life to defeat you: God has provided victory. You can face every trial... every circumstance... every problem without fear. Because you know God's ultimate purpose is to do you GOOD, He is in control of ALL your circumstances, and with every circumstance comes the provision for total victory! Your faith may presently be tested and tried, as gold is tried in a furnace. But, you are going to be able to stand firm, regardless of the circumstances that come to defeat you. Like Job, who was able to say in the midst of his fiery trials, "Though he slay me, yet will I trust in Him," Job 13:15.

God, Himself, is building a better you! Trust Him in the process!

"Now thanks be unto God, which always causeth us to triumph in Christ," 2 Corinthians 2:14.

6
Uncommon Achievers

Playing sports of any kind has an uncanny way of teaching you life skills. By cohesively physically and mentally working out, you have the opportunity to develop inner strength for life's mental toughness. This is a requirement needed in order to be persistent in any endeavor. You could draw experiences to use in your career, business, and personal relationships, as well as emotional stability. One of the main advantages of practicing a sport is the ability to develop coping skills with others. Athletes also learn how to work as a team. Learning the elements of hard work, and training are vital in forging ahead.

Athletes have developed self-confidence and acquired the necessary skills to eliminate distractions. As in any goal, there are always the possibilities of being distracted in your pursuit. Every obstacle athletes encounter on the field, in the ring, or in any arena, is crammed with conflicting, enormous decisions. Frequently, athletes are questioning themselves, "Will this sacrifice really pay off? Is the hard work really worth my efforts?" Because of the massive time dedicated to becoming their best, competitors spend a great deal just conditioning and practicing. Each time, aiming to do it better than the last time and targeting for full perfection.

This was the case of Frederick Fay, a man I read about in the Los Angeles Times obituary section. As a young man, he had a zest for sports, particularly basketball. I believe it was his love for basketball, whereby, he created a "no-quit" attitude. When he was in high school, Fay would shoot baskets for endless hours in his Bethesda, Maryland backyard. He was a baller determined to perfect his shots. Later, he would perform his routine of flips on a trapeze. Unfortunately, on one particular day, his visibly "normal routine" of basketball followed by gymnastics didn't have a favorable outcome.

With hands slick with sweat from shooting baskets, Fay only completed two flips. While on his third flip attempt, he lost his grip and fell 10 feet, breaking his neck in two places. At 16, Fay was a quadriplegic. Although Fay was now disabled, he refused to let his physical impairments define him.

Amazingly at 17, Fay co-founded a support network for the disabled. He went on to organize demonstrations and lobbying, which became the major precedent in winning support for the Federal Americans with Disabilities Act of 1990. This Act guarantees jobs for the disabled. Defying doctors' grim predictions for his survival, Fay was a leading activist for 50 years, until his death this past September 2011. Remarkably, Fay conducted most of his advocacy work while lying flat on his back.

More than 30 years ago, Fay was diagnosed with an inoperable spinal cyst. This condition inhibited his breathing and swallowing. Nonetheless, there was no stopping Fay. He staged an ingenious command center in his home. Computer monitors were mounted on the ceiling; he had a motorized bed, and strategically-placed mirrors surrounding his bed enabling him to continue working for his cause. I believe that Fay was so committed to his cause, that he had identified his purpose while laying flat on his back. His cause had become bigger than his disability.

Fay's cause was powerful enough to keep him looking up from even a bedridden position. His unyielding cause gave him the determination to unite with others with similar disadvantages. His cause, enabled him to sacrifice beyond the call of duty. When you're confronted by the Goliaths in your life, what is it that makes you want to attack? Your first step should be to identify and examine your cause.

Many fellow activists had no idea he was prostrate 24 hours-a-day. Those who did know, say his brilliance never ceased to amaze them. Somehow, Fay was able to locate the force of courage within him. Courage can be simply defined as an untiring and undefeatable attitude, born out of determination.

Advancements come through small increments of successes. You can never discount the diminutive scale of improvements. It is the combination of the tiny steps and the mundane practices that causes you to reach the top of the mountain. Every individual with determination has a mountain to climb. Sir Edmund Hillary, the first man who climbed to the top of Mount Everest, the highest mountain in the world, must have had a fierce amount of determination. He and his colleagues continually made several unsuccessful attempts at conquering the mountain. I'm fairly certain they must have left home each day with a camera packed in their gear, knowing surely this is the day they would make history.

> *Advancements come through small increments of successes.*

Numerous mornings were spent waving "good bye" to family and friends – all the while – a gleam in their eyes spoke victory. Unfortunately, Hillary and the rest of his hiking team returned home by the end of day, exhausted after covering an expansive portion of the mountain. Weary and disappointed, because the camera had not a trace of the film that would witness their triumphant accomplishment, Hillary was all but ready to give up.

Nevertheless, they would be back at it again the next morning with a mightier resolve and courage for the conquest. The mountaineers saddled their gear, which somehow began to feel heavier than the day before. With a slight breath of exertion, they inhaled the early morning breeze that somehow caused their exertion to dissipate. Wow! Once again, they were up for the day's challenge. Performing their normal routine, the men said their usual "good-byes." However, the gleam in the eyes of Hillary's team of hikers that once spoke victory now began to weaken.

For some, the adventurous climb seemed to get more difficult with each step up the mountain scope. While looking at the footprints that were left in the snow from the day before, their exorbitant desire to reach the top never exited from their minds. Weary in their bodies, yet more determined than ever, these hikers possessed the mental fortitude necessary to accomplish this journey. Consequently, it was not enough to take them to the top of the mountain.

Finally, Hillary and another climber who had both participated in five previous Everest trips were the only members of the hiking expedition able to make the final assault on the summit. So, at 11:30 on the morning of May 29, 1953, Edmund Hillary and his colleague reached the summit at 29,028 feet above sea level. This is the highest spot on earth.

While being interviewed, Hillary made an interesting statement. He said, "The modern mountaineers, with their very good technical equipment and their very accomplished techniques, can climb more naturally and easily than we did in our day. But of course, we had one problem that the modern mountaineer doesn't have. That is, the psychological barrier. We really didn't know whether it was humanly possible to reach the top of Mt. Everest."

But one day, Hillary stood before the mountain and spoke to it. On that specific day, he became bigger than the mountain. Consider what Mark 11:23 says:

> "For verily I say unto you, that whosoever shall say unto this mountain, be thou removed, and be thou cast into the sea, and shall not doubt in his heart, but

shall believe that those things which he saith shall come to pass, he shall have whatsoever he saith."

As a person hears the Word of God, the spirit of courage is being planted in their hearts. Therefore, when you speak the Word to yourself, you are injecting courage into yourself. Fear sets in when a man is quiet. Matter of fact, the quieter you are, the more fearful you will become. Speak to yourself, surroundings, and circumstances. Declare the Word concerning your life and situations. "If thou faint in the day of adversity, thy strength is small," (Proverbs 24:10).

> *As a person hears the Word of God, the spirit of courage is being planted in their hearts.*

When you are approaching a battle, going to a new venture or about to take a new step in life, one thing you need for success is a reflection of past victories. Literally, sit down and write out your past victories. Testimonies are like seeds: they germinate and grow. The more you testify and share your accomplishments, the more you have to give.

The Bible says, "You will reap, what you sow," (see Galatians 6:7). Therefore, the more victories I share, the more of a harvest I will be qualified to receive. Actually, you need to schedule "Victory Reports" on your calendar. Choose a day of the week, that you plan to share with friends, family members, and new acquaintances, of the goodness of God in your life. Testimonies are a powerful weapon for turning on the switch of courage.

Let's look at a powerful biblical lesson. Goliath had kept all Israel in bondage for 40 days. Saul, the king, had lost his backbone. But, here comes David, a youth of 17 that was speaking with an empowering type of boldness in I Samuel 17:32-36;

> Let no man's heart fail because of him (Goliath); thy servant will go and fight with this Philistine.

> David began to testify. ... "Thy servant kept his father's sheep, and there came a lion, and a bear, and took a lamb out of the flock.
>
> And I went out after him, and smote him, and delivered it out of his mouth: and when he arose against me, I caught him by his beard, and smote him, and slew him.
>
> Thy servant slew both the lion and the bear: and this uncircumcised Philistine shall be as one of them, seeing he had defied the armies of the living God.

David's testimony of the bear and the lion is how he turned on the switch of courage. People who have the courage to go forward when faced with challenges will never be short of testimonies. Consider David's strength from his own testimony as he spoke.

David envisioned Goliath as a dead man right from the outset. This is the reason he ran towards the Philistine when the time approached to lock horns. I encourage you to look into the eyes of your Goliath and envision whatever is trying to defeat you as dead. When something is dead, it has no ability to rule you, it has no governing power over you, and it just doesn't exist. It's your time to pull down your Jericho walls and behead your Goliaths!

Here is another compelling message. Your understanding of God's presence is pivotal in your quest for courage. You are settled when you carry His presence. Elisha is a very good example of one who carried His presence. When faced with a siege, he remained cool and relaxed. What was his secret? His consciousness of God's presence with him made him undaunted even in the face of imminent danger (2 Kings 6:13-17).

Jesus assured us of His continual presence with us before His ascension in Matthew 28:20. He said, ".. Lo, I am with you always.." David said in Psalm 23:4, "Yea, I walk through the valley of the shadow of death, I will fear no evil: for thou art with me."

The three Hebrew boys, Shadrach, Meshach and Abednego were courageous enough to go into the fire, because they were sure that God was with them. Whatever, you may be facing today, you must know it hasn't the ability to overtake and overthrow you. The fire of God is a consuming fire, and it will extinguish everything that has come to distinguish you!

I remember attending a crusade shortly after I got saved. The evangelist called for those who wanted to experience the power of God. Reluctantly, my mom and I ran to the altar, along with hundreds of others. Little did I realize, I would be different when I returned to my seat. The fire of God met us at that altar! I could sense the fire of God burning up things that had been lodged in my old nature. To this day, I'm unaware of all He did for me on that night. But, my life has never been the same.

Wake up in the morning declaring the Word of God over your life. Bold declarations infuse and induce courage into you. The more you speak, the more courageous you become. Words are a source of unseen energy. It generates a powerful force within the soul. Therefore, what you say is a formidable weapon for you to acquire whatever you need, whatever needs to be mended, and whatever is lost that needs to be found.

David spoke the defeat of Goliath into being, and all the angelic hosts came to his aid. With supernatural speed, he slung his slingshot and arrow! Goliath was down! In I Samuel 17:46, David declared:

> "This day will the Lord deliver thee into mine hand; and I will smite thee, and take thine head from thee; and I will give the carcasses of the host of the Philistines this day unto the fowls of the air."

Your words are the fuel of your life. The surest way to arrest whatever is trying to master you is through the power of speech. Let's practice, repeat after me, "Greater is He that is in me than he that is in the world." Words are powerful. Announce to yourself daily, "No weapon formed against me will ever prosper," (Isaiah 54:17). By the way, you don't need the applause of men to accomplish your God-given vision,

> *The fruits in your life are produced by your tongue.*

all you need is courage. The Bible says that every man shall be satisfied with the fruit of his lips (Proverbs 18:20).

The fruits in your life are produced by your tongue. Your fruits cannot be sweeter than your speech. If you have bitter fruits, it is because your tongue is bitter. The ten spies said in Numbers 13:27-29:

> ...We came unto the land whither thou sentest us, and surely it floweth with milk and honey...
>
> Nevertheless the people are strong that dwell in the land. The cities are walled, and very great: and moreover we saw the children of Anak there.
>
> The Amalekites dwell in the land of the south; and the Hittites, and the Jebusites, and the Amorites, dwell in the mountains: and the Canaanites dwell by the sea, and by the coast of Jordan.

The works of the enemy in our own personal lives today are similar to the heathen tribes, which the children of Israel had to conquer in order to claim their rightful inheritance. Thus, let's make a few declarations:

The Hittites: This word means, "fear" or "terror." I declare over your life right now that the spirit of fear is broken!

The Jebusites: This word means "to trample," and implies depression or oppression. I decree over you right now that the garment of praise expels a spirit of heaviness. Begin now to take a praise break! Praise silences the enemies of God which brings oppression. If God is for you, who can be against you?

The Amorites: This word means, "To speak or say," and implies negative speech. I declare and decree over your life right now that you will discipline your mind to meditate on that which is good, true, honest, just, pure, lovely and of a good report!

The Canaanites: This word literally means "to press down" or "to humiliate." I declare over you right now that oppression is far from you. Depression will not defeat nor conquer you!

They were expressing their experiences, instead of speaking their expectations. You must learn to declare your expectations always, like Joshua and Caleb, and not to explain your experience. They said, "Let us go up at once, and possess it; for we are well able to overcome it." As long as you keep declaring your experiences, your opportunities will close up. It is your expectations that open up your opportunities!

It's time to dethrone your enemies and concentrate on your opportunities. Speak less of what is working against you and talk more of what is working for you. Let your speech bring you your desired fruit!

God will neither resist nor oppose your speech. He has clearly said that what you say is what you get, (Numbers 14:28). Your speech creates your future. What you say now will definitely happen in your future; so, say ONLY what you want to see.

We can define courage also as strength to stand against the odds of life. Both Frederick Fay and Sir Edward Hillary demonstrated exceptional amounts of courage and beat the odds. Basically, it's an issue of the heart. It {courage} manifested in outward steps of bravery and boldness.

Both of these athletes had the ability to take steps in the face of imminent opposition, obstacles, hardships and difficulties. Their ceaseless, unremitting efforts kept them on their purposeful journeys. Let's face it. Most people have pipe dreams. But these two men of courage didn't have a pipe dream. They were both driven by a real cause. We learned from the lives of these two extraordinary men that courage is not subjective to the environment. Neither does it cower to public opinion. It's your turn and time to make something happen in your life. Do something, try something, and start taking action!

7
The Excuse Bag

The first excuse ever told was in the Garden of Eden. Now consider this for a moment, of all the places for an excuse to be birthed: why there? Spectacular creations of pure, exquisite beauty surrounded the garden. Sheer luminosity filled the atmosphere, where not a twinkle of darkness could be found. It was magnificence within the flora and glorious aroma of God's love and splendor. Its lush, green grass glistened among a colorful patch full of roses, azaleas, daisies, tulips, and other foliage, plants and trees new to humanity. The pathways between the orchids and sunflowers were surrounded by sand-like petals that sparkled. Every direction imaginable was a breathtaking view.

God's most precious garden had bounteous acres of shrubbery in every color. The blooming lily field was an endless meadow of heavenly radiance that lit up the grounds as beacons of light. Shades of blues and greens from the river that watered Eden were an unfailing flow of nourishment for vegetation. And peaceful tranquility covered the garden as blankets of love and security.

Unfortunately, here is where the problem begins. According to Genesis 2:8 and 9:

"And the LORD God planted a garden eastward in

Eden; and there he put the man whom he had formed. And out of the ground made the LORD God, to grow every tree that is pleasant to the sight, and good for food; the tree of life also in the midst of the garden, and the tree of knowledge of good and evil.

And the LORD God commanded the man, saying, 'of every tree of the garden thou mayest freely eat. But of the tree of the knowledge of good and evil, thou shalt not eat of it: for in the day that thou eatest thereof shalt surely die," (Genesis 2:16, 17).

As we all know, the serpent beguiled Eve, and she ate of the forbidden tree. She proceeded to give Adam the fruit, and he did eat. When God approached them about their disobedience, this was their response, according to Genesis 3:12, 13:

"And the man said, 'The woman whom thou gavest to be with me, she gave me of the tree, and I did eat. And the Lord God said unto the woman, what is this that thou hast done? And the woman said, the serpent beguiled me, and I did eat."

Neither of them was willing to take responsibility for their actions. Or, in other words, we could say they weren't willing to "own" up. Consequently, excuses have become part of the human race.

In order to eliminate excuses, we have to be willing to take personal accountability for our responsibility. An important aspect of responsibility is being personally accountable for our thoughts, words, attitudes, and actions.

- Responsibility for thoughts.

    "Casting down imaginations and every high thing that exalteth itself against the knowledge of God, and bringing into captivity every thought to the obedience of Christ," (II Corinthians 10:5).

The Excuse Bag

- Responsibility for words.

  "Every idle word that men shall speak, they shall give account thereof in the day of judgment. For by thy words thou shall be justified, and by thy words thou shalt be condemned," (Matthew 12:36-37).

- Responsibility for actions.

  "For we must all appear before the judgment seat of Christ; that every one may receive the things done in his body, according to that he hath done, whether it be good or bad," (II Corinthians 5:10).

- Responsibility for attitudes.

  "Keep thy tongue from evil and thy lips from speaking guile," (Psalm 34:13).

During one of our "Winner's Circle" Bible Study, we explored the importance of taking responsibility. This particular Women's Bible Study group also looked at not blaming others for personal misfortunate circumstances. For so long, many of us have avoided claiming responsibility for our own unfulfilled destinies. Both intentionally and unintentionally, we grow up, leave home and continue to point the finger at others for all our issues, setbacks and insecurities. Spouses, bosses, relatives and friends are faulted for our excess baggage.

> *In order to eliminate excuses, we have to be willing to take personal accountability for our responsibility.*

However, in order to move on from certain irresponsible behavior, we must face the challenges that makes us want to quit and make excuses. As long as you are accusing your opponent, you can't do anything to change the problem. For example, someone that is drowning in the ocean must become a participant in his own rescue. Otherwise, the rescue efforts are more difficult. If the potential drown victim continues to fight to survive, instead of allowing the rescuer to do his job, then both are in danger. Drowning victims are probably the most dangerous to try to rescue. The sufferer's natural instinct is to claw at the rescuers. However, she fails to realize that the power to overcome is in her own hands.

Surviving also requires self-participation. If you accept the disillusionment that there is nothing you can do about your circumstances, you have then become a victim – chained to your current life. Living life as a spiritual and emotional vagabond: you become a leach to everyone within reach of your claws.

Nevertheless, your deliverance from making excuses comes by taking ownership of your own predicament; refuse to play the "blame game," and taking full responsibility of your life! You have created the present, but you can also recreate your future!

> *Courage gives you the ability to persevere and continue on the journey once it's started.*

None of this is accomplished without courage, which is the unwavering and undefeatable attitude, born out of determination. A significant part of courage is the ability to take steps in the face of opposition, hardship and difficulty. Courage gives you the ability to persevere and continue on the journey once it's started. With courage, you possess the ability to maintain your positive confession: even when circumstances may warrant that you change your beliefs.

Determination is looking at insurmountable obstacles and setbacks as opportunities to see the supernatural intervention of God. Deliberately and precisely is how Moses demonstrated determination: instead of opting out with an excuse. When he chose to suffer affliction with the children of Israel rather than enjoy the pleasures of sin, Moses could have chosen the lesser road of resistance. But, no! Moses didn't fall into the trap of explanations. Rather, Moses chose to obey God and suffer with the children of Israel. He recognized that, "the approach of Christ brought greater riches than the treasures in Egypt: for he had respect unto the recompense of the reward," (Hebrews 11:26).

The truth of the matter is that we have all made excuses. We have even learned to beautify them with sparkling glitter, rhinestones, and shiny, shimmering colors. Some are more subtle, concealed, and tucked away than others. In order for explanations to travel with us everywhere we go, we've designed a shoulder strap purse or man-bag that's tailor-made for our personal needs. Besides, comfort and convenience is the only way to travel. Furthermore, it would be a pure shame to have left home without our prized possessions. Surely, how could we survive without having at least one or two excuses tucked away? Just in case we needed it for the day's activities. Wow! Living life without excuses: who in the world has heard of such a thing?

Now, let's pick back up on the story of Adam and Eve. Unbeknownst to them when they made the decision to obey the serpent rather than God: the first man and woman set off a debilitating domino effect. The Bible gives the account in Genesis 4:1-10 of the first murder that would take place in history. Cain was jealous of his brother's offering to the Lord and decided to kill him. Of course, when asked by God regarding the whereabouts of his brother, Cain replied with a question, "Am I my brother's keeper?"

The mere statement was indicative of Cain's selfish and self-centered nature. When it came down to caring for others, he would always make an excuse. These types of character traits are adverse to the teachings of God. His intent for man was to care for and meet the needs of one another. Excuses reveal a person's core value as well as an individual's lack of character. Oftentimes, people who use a lot of explanations operate in laziness, jealousy, pride and competitiveness. For example, Cain's pride interfered with him doing and putting his best efforts forward. Because, his efforts and sacrifice weren't accepted, Cain's pride got the best of him.

Your core story has helped define who you are today. I'm fairly certain that Cain had previously exemplified a history of being competitive with his brother in the past. This trait didn't "suddenly" appear. Somehow, along the way, Cain had gotten stuck, justifying his misery, fear and dysfunction.

What past belief or experience is fueling your insecurity? Now, more than ever, it is clearly apparent that insecurity is becoming a worldwide epidemic. Insecurity has caused us to question our; looks, performance, careers, judgment and, even deliberations about life. Its incapacitating effect has become our worst enemy.

Lack of confidence hides behind the excuses; "If only I had a better up-bringing," "I should have been born into another family," "My father should have been there for me," and "If only I had a higher education." The list goes on. Matter of fact, let's get real, I've heard a few of them echo from my own vocal chords from time to time. Plus, I'm writing not because I have arrived, or have become an expert on the subject matter. The truth and nothing but the truth is, I'm just like you: striving to eliminate excuses from my own terminology.

To be honest, I'm just an ordinary woman, sharing ordinary problems. But, I'm on an extraordinary journey with a supernatural Deliverer. After all, "No trial has overtaken us that is not faced by others. And God is faithful," (I Corinthians 10:13, NET).

On another note, since I just had a flashing thought, allow me to share more. It's off the subject a bit, but it bears being said. Quite often, men and women are less attracted to persons that are overly emotional and possess low self-esteem. Consequently, there is nothing that is irresistible about that package of curves and biceps. No matter what shape or size. Life has its own challenges. For me to choose a life-partner that I have to coach and motivate every waking moment of the day is insane.

Circumstances change in a hot second. Obstacles and setbacks aren't just for the elite and famous. Nor is it for the hard-pressed, weak and fragile. Career changes are warranted. Betrayals and abandonment have become household words. I bring this up to demonstrate, I don't need a needy or insecure person all up in my space.

Some of us have learned to look outside ourselves for security: instead of looking within for that God-given ability and fortitude to become all we are meant to be.

With two voices inside one body speaking simultaneously, it's time for the "real" one to take a stand. The voice of hope that has found its security in his or her God-ordained temple should be the loudest, and speak with authority. When the power of God is intact, nothing can make you feel insecure. OK. Point made. Let's proceed.

> *Some of us have learned to look outside ourselves for security: instead of looking within for that God-given ability and fortitude to become all we are meant to be.*

Cain's scanty excuse did not go well with God. He was then cursed from the land of his parents. His lot in life would be a fugitive and vagabond in the earth. All this transpired because Cain chose to lean towards his human nature side. Think about it. Both Cain and Abel were raised in the same home. I'm sure they heard numerous stories about the decision their parents had made in Eden regarding listening to the serpent, and disobeying God. But subsequently, one of them still made a horrendous decision. That one abominable choice changed the whole history of which the Bible was to be written and read today.

Excuses are like shortcuts, offering you the flexibility to avoid going the distance. Such justifications often prevent you from accomplishing what is necessary to being successful. Additionally, it takes sacrifice to be victorious. Excuses will cause you to avoid making the necessary adjustments.

Unbeknownst to him at the time, Jesse sabotaged his career and forfeited his opportunity of earning a position on The Alliance Soccer Team for his home state of Washington. Because of a few wrong decisions, Jesse's promising career that began when he was only 11 slowly evaporated right before his eyes. Jesse's natural talent and eagerness was the perfect combination to explode on the soccer field. Growing up, Jesse had set his goals of someday traveling throughout the state of Washington with his teammates. What an accomplishment he imagined, doing what he most enjoyed. After all, Jesse was convinced playing soccer was his purpose in life.

However, Jesse's eagerness wasn't enough to secure him a position on the soccer team. His unwillingness to continually sacrifice the long strenuous hours of tireless practice was beginning to surface; not only to himself, but to his teammates as well. Coach Roberts also began to notice Jesse's uncommitted work ethics. He had worked with Jesse for almost four years, and recently noticed Jesse displaying a lackluster attitude for the past few months. Unfortunately, the enthusiasm Jesse once cherished was slowly dissipating, like a lingering leakage from an unnoticeable tire hole.

Likewise, many people work excessively hard to accomplish their goals. But, along the way, they face numerous obstacles. Eventually, some forfeit their potential. Ultimately, losing all their zeal and pursuit, they begin to fill up their "excuse bag." I'm sure Jesse's bag was filled with invisible statements like; "What's the use?," "I'm tired," and "No one appreciates me," just to name a few.

The longer you remain in the game, irregardless if you're not the most talented or skilled on the team – the more likely you are to regain positioning. Nevertheless, the more likely you are to dominate whatever is trying to dominate you. It's time, not only to empty your excuse bag, but throw it away once and for all!

"For no temptation, has overtaken you, and laid hold on you that is not common to man. But with the temptation He will always also provide the way out the means of escape to a landing place that you may be capable and strong and powerful to bear up under it patience," (I Corinthians 10:13) AMP.

8
The Football Game

On the way to our seats, my husband and I hiked up several colorful rows of bleachers. While occasionally gazing down into a marvelous stream of fans wearing their favorite blue, orange and white sports attire, it was clearly evident. We were smack in the middle of a high school football showdown. Bullhorns, cowbells, whistles and noisemakers battled for attention during the pre-game football frenzy. The zesty aroma of pizza, hot dogs, chili and coffee floated from the snack bar.

Although I was bundled up in a heavy jacket, it still felt nippy as my nose adjusted to the crisp night air. I sustained my mantra during the hike, "Excuse me. Excuse me please." Reluctantly, my husband and I continued taking steps in fear of accidentally stepping on someone or someone's belongings. Fortunately, we finally maneuvered our way to our landing space, and took our seats. We were nestled among a tremendous gathering of fans. Obviously, there was no need to ask, "Where is my team sitting?"

Just across the field, you could find bleachers filled with a cavalry of fans wearing burgundy, white and gold. These two teams had a long history, of being rivals in the adjoining cities. Parents had come prepared for a much-anticipated game. Family fans were loaded down with their seat cushions, memorabilia, snacks and blankets for the breezy night air. By the intense rage of excitement, you could've easily mistaken some of the fans for players on the field. In fact, on both a mental and emotional level, some of these fans were "for real" about being on the field in their minds and from the looks of things.

A sense of energy electrified the stadium the moment the announcer came on the loud speaker. Folks popped up to attention, becoming more intense and alert. All eyes focused on the humongous lighted, football field. Both school cheerleader squads began performing and hyping the crowd, along with their respective marching bands. It was showtime and the football teams were preparing to exit their locker rooms, which were adjacent to the playing field. Each team would have their golden opportunity to make their own grand entrance.

Running through the banner, each team member was like a shooting arrow. He was focusing strictly on annihilating the opposing team. The camaraderie between the team players was exceptional. They gave each other "high-fives," and passed along a look of determination and fearlessness in their eyes. Parents, relatives and friends were cheering the players on in hopes of boosting their ego and reaffirming their unbeatable stance.

It had been a while since we had attended a high school football game. Thus, my husband and I find it amazing how personal and serious some parents and supporters take these games. Consequently, we buckled our seatbelts and prepared to witness an array of emotions from team boosters. As they sat close together like a hive of bees, we could hear both appalling and comical responses which surely proved to be the norm of the evening's event.

Well, with a tied score, and less than a minute left on the time clock, we were forced into overtime. The attendees were on their feet as the two team captains flipped the coin to determine who would be receiving the ball. The coin was flipped and the game began. As I watched the football game on that evening, I learned a few life lessons that I will be writing about in this portion of the chapter.

First and foremost, football is an interesting and strategic sport. When confronted with various adversities and crisis in our lives, we also must be strategic in our approach. Now, before I begin tackling this portion of the chapter, I must admit, I'm an amateur in the sport. So please, bear with me.

The goal of the offensive strategy is to score points. To successfully accomplish this goal, coaches and players must execute specific plays based on a variety of factors including; the skill of the players, the opponent's defensive strategy, amount of time remaining before halftime, or time remaining until the end of the game. Strategically, the offense can also be used to prevent the opponent from scoring points by denying the opponent possession of the ball.

The goal of the defensive strategy is to prevent the opposing offense from gaining yards and scoring points. Defensive players can do this either by preventing the offensive line from advancing the ball beyond the line of scrimmage or by the defensive players taking the ball away (intercepting) from the offense and scoring points themselves.

Formations for both the offensive and defensive strategies are different. Teams often have special formations that they may have developed for that particular game or sometimes just to confuse the defense. Again, the defensive squad's aim is to neutralize their opponent's strength. Therefore, many hours of reviewing footage from their opposing team is extremely crucial. Reviewing the other team's weaknesses as well as their strengths gives them the upper-hand and advantage on game day. By studying their plays, they become aware of possible plays, as well as predictable players they might utilize in that particular play.

At the end of the game, the team that normally wins is the one that strategically planned for every possible setback or obstacle imaginable. Another major factor in winning is the team that has mastered playing under pressure knows how to deal with frustration, and best works in less than desirable conditions. Finally, a team strategically wins, by concentrating on one play at a time. Inch-by-inch, foot-by-foot, they move down the field, and as they do, eventually, they get to the end zone. If they are thinking about the end zone every second, they will drop the ball. So, their efforts are calculated one play at a time.

Conversely, your life has similar circumstances and will present obstacles that you must overcome. An obstacle can be considered a barrier, action or situation that causes an obstruction. It creates a difficulty, nuisance or disorder to achieve concrete goals. Without a strategic plan to bounce back from a setback, and become proficient in handling pressure, you will constantly be living at the mercy of your challenge. Consequently, you must push through every comfort barrier. Success in winning is based on pushing through comfort obstructions, shattering fears of failure and success, and breaking glass ceilings. Pushing through pain and obstacles is one of the most valuable lessons a person can master in life.

> *Without a strategic plan to bounce back from a setback, and become proficient in handling pressure, you will constantly be living at the mercy of your challenge.*

I need for you to take a moment, close your eyes, and envision yourself crossing the finish line with your hands in the air like winners do. Envision yourself running the whole way: not slowing down your pace, but continuing forward. Keep pressing- even if you're tired or if you're in pain. Practicing these empowering thoughts will keep you moving in the face of obstacles and setbacks.

"As a man thinketh so is he."

What images are in your mind today, regarding the obstacle you are facing? One evening at our weekly, "Winners Circle" Bible

Study, I posed a similar question to the women. What obstacles are you facing? One of the ladies responded that her biggest obstacle is saying, "NO!" She went on to express, that she spends numerous hours a day, rehearsing in her mind, "Why am I allowing people to take advantage of me and becoming bitter and angry at the choices I have made?"

She has become so consumed with negative thinking that all she can imagine is defeat and hopelessness. Instead of meditating on how she plans to overcome this obstacle and take immediate action, her mind is stuck rehearsing reruns of defeat. She sees one episode after another, pushing the replay button throughout the day. The woman has become accustomed to using her imagination in a negative way. Imagination is the formation of mental pictures or images.

We have a tendency to ultimately become like that which we imagine or envision ourselves to be. If we imagine ourselves as failing, we are more likely to fail. Imagination has the ability to form mental pictures, to visualize irritating or fearful situations in concrete form. Once we perceive a feeling and begin to think about it, the imagination goes to work. The imagination reinforces the thoughts, which intensify the feelings. You can always trace a feeling you are expressing by the thoughts you are thinking. Remember, everything in life starts with a thought.

As we hold onto those sabotaging thoughts it seeps into our subconscious and eventually becomes a "fixed" image in our minds. My homework assignment for her was to say, "NO" before she returned next week to class. You can create first-rate, protective fences with your words. By saying, "No" you are establishing a solid boundary. You are informing others that you exist apart from them and that you are in control of you.

Another woman within the group articulated that one of her major challenges was worrying about the security of her job. To worry actually means to strangle or choke. When we worry, we are strangling or choking our emotions. We block any flow of creativity. Worrying also paralyzes us, and causes us to focus on events and circumstances that are beyond our control. It is really an attempt to control our future. If we are worrying about our job, then we are saying that one of the major objects of trust for our future is our job. Or, if we are worrying about money, we are placing our faith for the future in money.

Your worries identify your "security blanket" for the future. Think about it. A blanket or toy carried by a child is designed to reduce or dispel anxiety. We are walking around with our invisible "security blankets" in hopes of finding temporary consolation and artificial assurance. The key to breaking the paralyzing cycle of worry and anxiety is to find something dependable in which to trust. Fortunately, the only thing worth trusting is God, Himself.

"No one can serve two masters; for either he will hate the one and love the other, or he will be devoted to the one, and despise the other. "You cannot serve God and manna," (Matthew 6:24).

You cannot trust God for the future, and at the same time worry about not having enough money or whatever the need may be.

"Blessed are all those who put their trust in Him," (Psalm 2:12). Many times, obstacles are disguised as hidden possibilities. Limitless resources are at your disposal but you may have to dig deeper than the obstruction to grasp the possibility. In my own personal life, there have been great lessons learned: right beyond the challenge. My focus was so much on the problem that I couldn't see the answer. Right now, you may not be able to see your possibilities, but I guarantee they are there to be found.

Start exploring. Begin plowing through the dirt. Focus on the goal, and its resources are right in close proximity. All obstacles of life have stairs attached to them. Now is the time to step up and out of your dilemma. Unfortunately, you cannot escape problems, but you can take a mental break, and reevaluate the situation. When you take another look from a different perspective, somehow it looks a lot smaller. On occasion, when I'm upset, there is a tendency for me to hear with a bad attitude.

Have you ever had someone attempt to console you, but you felt like you were being attacked? They were doing their best to comfort you. Instead, you refused to listen. So often, when we are faced with unfavorable moments, we close our ears from our very help. Remove the earplugs and welcome your help.

God has assigned people in your life, for this season of your life, to assist you in coming through this obstacle. It is your depth of gratitude that determines your altitude. "In everything give thanks; for this is the will of God in Christ Jesus concerning you," (I Thessalonians 5:18). Ingratitude stops the intervention of the Holy Spirit; it pushes back the hand of God.

> "Cast not away therefore your confidence, which hath great recompense of reward. For ye have need of patience, that, after ye have done the will of God, ye might receive the promise," (Hebrews 10:35-36).

In the above Scripture, we find out that we can only receive the promise after we have done the will of God. And what is the will of God? "In everything, give thanks."

> *His presence is what renders your enemies helpless: paving a way for your glorious victory!*

Until the will of God is done, you cannot obtain the promise. So every pursuit in life, every obstacle that you must overcome ought to culminate in thanksgiving. Right now, let's take a "Praise Break." Lift up your hands to Him in thanksgiving; from the depths of your heart, and for all things-give Him thanks! His presence is your guarantee to bounce-back!

His presence is what renders your enemies helpless: paving a way for your glorious victory!

It's time for you to create an opportunity, if no one is coming to your aid, then you create one. The woman with the issue of blood said in her heart (through creative thinking), and out-of-the-box thinking, "There is no way I can get to this man, because of the crowd. If I may touch the hem of His garment, I will be made whole." She created an opportunity for her healing. You create opportunities through creative thinking. You have a God-given ability to create things. We are heirs of God and joint-heirs with Christ. You can make it happen! It's time to cut the umbilical cord of defeat from your life.

I read a story, years ago about a man named Karl Wallenda. He was a professional tightrope artist and founder of "The Flying Wallendas," a renowned family daredevil, stunt act. Matter of fact, his family members have been very successful in the circus business. Traveling around the world, performing in various circuses, was his family's passion. However, weeks prior to Karl taking his final tightrope walk, Karl's wife told some of their close friends that he began questioning his talent. This was totally out of character for Karl and, a bit surprising to her and those who worked closely with him. Karl would be seen checking and questioning the set-up of the performance, ensuring everything was done properly. He put all his energies into falling, rather than walking the tightrope.

On that dreaded day, Karl walked the tightrope with the fear of falling looming in his mind. This thinking created his feeling of insecurity. He had become consumed with falling, and that's exactly what happened. Here is a man that had grown-up performing on the tight-rope on a weekly basis for more than 40 years. But because he poured his energy into falling, his fear became his reality.

I haven't a clue who I may be ministering to right now. But you may be experiencing an apparently overwhelming barrier or difficulty in your life. The odds of success are outweighing the hope of a triumphant outcome. Well my friend, it's time for you to talk your way into success. The words of your mouth determine your outcome. It is impossible to encounter success without talking about success.

The words we speak are seeds. "The seed is the word of God," (Luke 8:11). Essentially, the amount of the Word of God that is spoken from your mouth in any area of your life, determines your harvest in that area. So, when you fill your heart with words of success, and express it through your mouth, you are sowing seeds of success. It's time for you to push open every door that is robbing you of total victory in your life.

> *It is impossible to encounter success without talking about success.*

No longer will you be paralyzed by doubts and fears. Today is your day to break the cycle! Get moving! Build momentum! Get back on the obstacle course of life! Get off the sidelines, and get back in the game! Throughout this book, you have heard numerous testimonies of challenging seasons. But, it was only for a season of time: before their test became their testimony. Your season of defeat has expired! No obstacle or setback will hold you back. You are BOUNCING-BACK!

Notes

Notes

Notes

Notes

Notes

Notes

Notes

Bibliography

Achievement.org/autodoc/SirEdmun Hillary Interview, 30 Sept. 2011.

English Standard Translation of the Bible

King James Version of the Bible

New Living Translation of the Bible

The Oxford Dictionary

The Vine's Complete Expository Dictionary of Old and New Testament Words

Wikipedia.org/wiki/Americanfootballstrategy. 17 Oct. 2011

Wikipedia.org/wiki/Obstacle. 18 Oct. 2011

Wikipedia.org/wiki/Survivor (TV Series). 3 Sept. 2011.

Wikipedia.org/wiki/Karl_Wallenda. 9 Nov. 2011

Wikipedia.org/wiki/Wipeout (TV Series). 15 Jul. 2011

Bishop, Rochelle. Personal Interview. 15 Aug. 2011

Folk, Jackie. Personal Interview. 15 Aug. 2011

Scott, Angela. Personal Interview. 28 Aug. 2011.

Woo, Elaine. "Frederick A. Fay dies at 66; advocate for rights of the disabled." Los Angeles Times. 4 Sep. 2011.

Linda Hodge

Linda G. Hodge is a wife, mother, grandmother, pastor, motivational speaker, and now she adds the title of author. For more than a decade, Linda has produced conferences, seminars, and extreme makeovers designed to uplift, support and empower women with the tools to renovate and restore their God-given purpose in life. Her commitment to abused women and children is unwavering. By popular demand, and encouragement, Linda was inspired to write her self-help manual, Woman Under Construction to help bring more women to a place of healing and success.

Linda G. Hodge co-pastors Living Praise Christian Center with her husband, Dr. Fred L. Hodge, Jr. in Chatsworth and Lancaster, California. The have five children and six grandchildren.

www.ingramcontent.com/pod-product-compliance
Lightning Source LLC
Chambersburg PA
CBHW071726040426
42446CB00011B/2235